The Making a Murderer Case

The Making a Murderer Case

Voices of True Crime
Book 2

Alan R. Warren

The Making a Murderer Case
Voices of True Crime Interviews Series: Volume 2
Written by Alan R. Warren
Published by House of Mystery

Cover design, formatting, layout, and editing by Evening Sky Publishing Services

Published in United States of America
ISBN (eBook): 978-1-989980-78-1
ISBN (Paperback): 978-1-989980-79-8

Contents

Part Five
INTERROGATION OF BRENDAN DASSEY

Introduction

The *House of Mystery Radio show* has been on the air for ten years, broadcasting in over a dozen cities in the U.S. It started as a way to interview guests knowledgeable in many of the world's mysteries involving crime, science, religion, history, paranormal, conspiracies, etc. A substantial number of our radio show's interviews revolve around true crime. So, we created this sub-series, *Voice of True Crime*, a curated collection of true crime interviews from the show. Each volume focuses on an actual criminal case, or several, providing the background and reproducing the main points discussed in the interviews. We review the most accepted explanation of the case. Then, we follow up with each theory presented during our interviews with the person or people reporting them.

Each book lays out the case details and then follows up with what we've learned from each guest. Like the others in the *House of Mystery Radio Show Interviews Series,* this book does not attempt to solve the case but only reviews it. There will be no committed answer at the end of the book. We aim to concisely review the extraordinary things we learned during the show's interviews.

These interview books are an excellent reference for researchers and a good overview for people who don't know the topic well. Only the highlights of each interview will be included; however, all these interviews and more are available on my website: www.alanrwarren.com/hom-podcast-episodes.

Volume two in the series covers the Teresa Halbach murder case, made famous from Netflix's *Making a Murderer* documentary series that began airing in December 2015. The *House of Mystery Radio Show* interviewed several of the key players involved in the case: Ken Kratz, the prosecutor of both Steven Avery and Brendan Dassey, and Michael Griesbach, District Attorney for Manitowoc Country who, after Steven Avery was wrongfully convicted in his first trial brought the misconduct of the law enforcement to the state's attorney. For the defense, we spoke with Laura Nirider from the Innocence Project, an expert in false convictions. We also interviewed Shawn Rech, a filmmaker that set out to correct the record on this murder case and expose the inaccuracies in the *Making a Murderer* series by creating his own docuseries coming early 2023 titled *Convicted*.

We also examine one of the major theories surrounding this murder case brought on by retired Detective John A. Cameron. Cameron wrote a book that is the center of a five-part A&E series suggesting that the crime was committed by someone who had nothing to do with any of the players involved in *Making a Murderer*. He asserts serial killer Edward Wayne Edwards committed the crime.

Part One

THE CASE

Chapter 1
Steven Avery

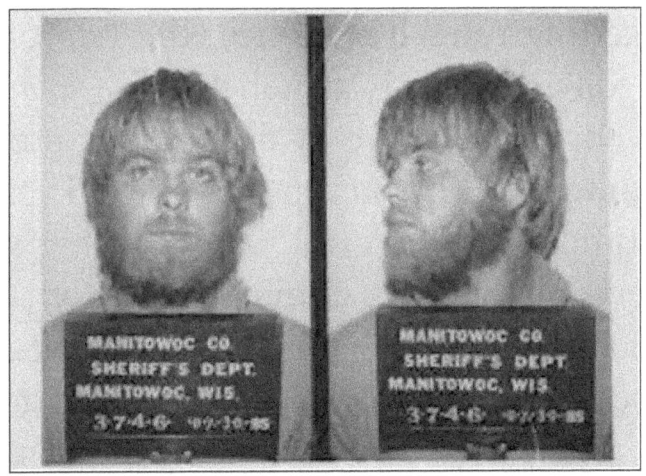

S teven Avery was born in Manitowoc County, Wisconsin, on July 9, 1962. His parents owned and operated a forty-acre salvage yard in Gibson, Wisconsin, in 1965, when Steven was only three years old. Steven had two brothers, Chuck and Earl, and one sister, Barb. All three of them went to school in Mishicot, where Steven was considered slower than the other kids in his class. Later in 1985, Avery's lawyer claimed that Steven only had an IQ of 70.

In the Spring of 1981, Steven and one of his school friends broke into a local tavern, where they destroyed most of the inside, robbed the gambling machines, and pocketed about fourteen dollars in quarters. They also took two sandwiches, a toolbox, and two cases of beer. After getting caught by police, the two of them were convicted and sentenced to spend ten months in jail, followed by five years of probation and a fine of $1399. Steven was only 18 years old at the time.

Avery kept up his criminal behavior. Only a few months after being released, he was at a barbeque party, and he was seen pouring gasoline on his family's cat and then throwing it into the bonfire at the party. He was arrested and charged with cruelty to animals. He denied doing anything to his cat but was convicted and sentenced to another nine months in jail.

Shortly after Steven turned 20 years old, on

July 29, 1982, he married Lori Mathiesen, a single mother of one son. They would have four other children together over the next three years, two girls, Rachel and Jenny, and twin boys, Steven Jr. and William. Everything seemed great between the couple until January 1985, when a woman named Sandra Morris, Steven's cousin, claimed he used to take his penis out and show it to her every time she drove by his house. After her complaint, Steven ran Morris off the road and then tried to kidnap her at gunpoint in his car. According to Morris, Steven only let her go after he realized that she had an infant in the back seat of her car. After he was arrested, he admitted to trying to run her off the road but denied having a gun. He was convicted of endangering another person's life and sentenced to six years in prison.

It was this assault case that led police to think that he could have also been the culprit of the rape and attempted murder of 36-year-old Penny Beerntsen on Two Rivers Beach. So, in July 1985, Steven was accused of sexually assaulting Penny Beerntsen, and he was eventually convicted and sentenced to 32 years in prison. However, this case was later overturned, and Avery was released after serving 18 years in prison.

Avery then sought millions in damages for wrongful imprisonment. Many considered his win to be the reason he was later charged and convicted of Teresa Halbach's murder.

In 1988, Lori filed for divorce from Steven, which caused even more trouble. Avery used to send her threatening letters from prison, telling her he would kill her and make her pay for divorcing him. After their divorce, Lori married Peter Dassey, the father of Brendan Dassey, who would later be convicted with Steven for the murder of Teresa Halbach. To make things even more complicated, Peter was previously married to Steven's sister Barb, who was Brendan's mother. So, Steven's ex-wife ended up being his nephew's stepmother.

The Penny Beerntsen Case

Penny was jogging near the Lake Michigan beach in July 1985 when she was attacked, assaulted, and raped. The victim picked Avery out as her attacker from a photo lineup while she was treated in the hospital after the attack. She later again identified Avery in a live lineup.

Even though Avery had sixteen witnesses

testifying that he was forty miles away in Green Bay during the attack and a receipt from a purchase he made there, he was charged and convicted.

The public believed that the police had a motive for going after Avery. This vendetta became obvious after discovering they were watching another suspect, Gregory A. Allen, for committing several assaults on the same beach where Beerntsen was attacked. Yet, they arrested Avery.

Their surveillance of Allen began in early August 1983 after he walked up to a woman, pulled his shorts down, and in front of her started to masturbate. While she stood in shock and started to scream, he jumped on her and tried to remove her clothing. She fought him off and ran away. Allen was later arrested and charged with the assault. After he found out the victim's identity, including her address and phone number from information given to him by his attorney, he started calling her, asking if she would drop the charges. Allen was convicted of disorderly conduct and released on probation after paying a fine.

The police started to get several complaints

from people living in the same beach area that a peeping Tom was looking through their windows or glass doors. In some of these cases, it was reported that even if the culprit was spotted by the homeowner and yelled at, he just stood in front of their window and masturbated. These reports made police in the neighborhood believe that Gregory Allen also did these offenses, but they had no proof. The police decided to assign a couple of officers to watch Allen twenty-four hours a day as they believed his actions might turn into physical assault or even rape.

On a hot summer afternoon at about 4 p.m. on July 29th, Penny Beerntsen was jogging along the shoreline of Lake Michigan when she first noticed a man wearing a leather jacket walking towards her. It seemed strange to wear such a heavy jacket to the beach on a hot summer day. When he was within a few feet of her, he drew a knife and told her to go into the nearby area with trees and shrubs. There he raped and beat her and left her for dead.

The police made their first error while visiting Beerntsen in the hospital. While Deputy Judy Dvorak questioned her about what had happened that afternoon, she received a basic description of her assailant. They planned to show Beerntsen a lineup of photos while she was still in the hospital to see if she could identify her attacker.

What's strange is that instead of thinking about Gregory Allen, who had been committing sexual offenses on the same beach and was already under surveillance by police, Dvorak immediately presumed the culprit was Steven Avery. Dvorak was friends with Sandra Morris—the woman Avery had run off the road a few years earlier—and her prejudging led police to add Avery's picture to the photo lineup. But they did not include Gregory Allen's photo. It's worth mentioning that Avery and Allen were very similar in looks and could easily be mistaken for each other.

When Beerntsen was released from the hospital, she was brought into the police station to view a live lineup of suspects. Again, Avery was there, but Allen was omitted, so she would never see him. Beerntsen picked Avery out of this lineup as well.

In December 1985, Avery went on trial. Even though he had a store receipt and sixteen witnesses who testified that they saw him in a ShopKo grocery store in Green Bay, about forty minutes away from the beach where the rape occurred, he was still convicted of the crime. On March 10, 1986, Avery was sentenced to 32 years for first-degree sexual assault and false imprisonment. He appealed his case twice, first in August 1987 and second in September 1996. Both cases were denied. Avery again appealed the 1996 denial the following year. He was unsuccessful, but he continued to maintain his innocence.

Another five years passed when, in April 2002, the Judge who denied Avery's appeal granted permission for the Wisconsin Innocence Project to conduct new DNA tests because of the advancements in this area of science. The Wisconsin crime lab retested thirteen of the hairs that had been recovered from Beerntsen back when the crime occurred in 1985. One of the hairs was a positive match for Allen, and none matched Avery. They also learned that Allen was serving prison time for a different rape he committed back in 1985 at the same beach.

On September 11, 2003, Avery was released from prison after serving eighteen years for a rape he didn't commit. He then returned to his parent's home and began working for them at their salvage yard. Within a year, Avery found a new girlfriend and moved into a trailer with her.

The Wisconsin Attorney General, Peg Lautenschlager, had the Justice Department investigate Avery's case but found no wrongdoing with their conduct or no ethics violations.

The following year in October 2004, Avery's attorney Walt Kelley filed a federal lawsuit against Manitowoc County, their former Sheriff Tom Kocourek, and District Attorney Denis Vogel of Madison County, which asked for thirty-six million dollars in damages. The lawsuit stated that the police ignored the obvious prime suspect, Gregory Allen, to get an indictment and conviction on Steven Avery.

The lawsuit trial started in October 2005 when several county officials, detectives, and county correctional officers gave depositions about the case from 1985. The lawsuit favored Avery, as he was imprisoned for eighteen years for a crime he didn't commit. It had been making the news cycles locally, statewide, and nationally.

By some coincidence, there was a television production company that was making a docuseries covering the original conviction of Steven Avery and the DNA that eventually overturned his conviction. They happened to be filming aspects of the lawsuit against the county for locking Avery up for eighteen years on a crime that he didn't commit. Little did they know that it wasn't going to end there. There would be a murder and many more trials to come that would captivate criminologists, fascinate the general population, and provide material for writers and filmmakers up to today.

Chapter 2
Murder of Teresa Halbach

Teresa Halbach was born and raised in Green Bay, Wisconsin, where she grew up working on her parent's dairy farm with her two brothers and sisters. Halbach graduated from the University of Wisconsin and loved to travel abroad to Mexico, Spain, and Australia. Halbach was twenty-five years old and loved photography so much that she started her own business by recording people's most important moments on film.

On Halloween 2005, online marketer Autotrader sent out Teresa Halbach, one of their photographers, to take pictures of a minivan that Barb Tadych from Manitowoc, Wisconsin, owned and wanted to sell through them. For Teresa, the Autotrader job was extra income while getting her business up and running. By the Fall of 2005, Teresa had acquired enough business to quit Autotrader, and this job on Halloween was supposed to be one of the last that she would do for them.

Barb Tadych was married to Scott Tadych and lived with him and her stepson, Brendan Dassey. Next to them lived Barb's brother, Steven Avery, who would eventually be convicted of Halbach's murder. Halbach had been on Tadych's property as many as fifteen times before to take other pictures for Autotrader, so she was familiar with the house and people there. This job was her fourth and last job that day. Sadly, she would never return home again.

After three days passed and her family was still unable to locate her, her parents, Tom and Karen, reported her missing. A search began the next day. At first, only four police officers were assigned to the Halbach missing person case. It didn't seem they were taking things too seriously until a volunteer group of searches spotted what looked like Halbach's RAV4 in Avery's Salvage Yard.

Detectives quickly arrived at the yard, had the vehicle removed, and sent it to the FBI crime lab in the capital of Wisconsin, Madison, to be analyzed. Now that Halbach's car was found, the police sent over two hundred officers to scour the Avery properties. The police found Halbach's spare key for her RAV4 lying in Steven Avery's bedroom on the carpet near his bed. Her license plate was found in a station wagon on the property. Then the most significant discovery was when a couple of human bones were seen near Avery's fire pit – where he would regularly have a fire burning while having friends over for beers.

The following week was a flurry of activity: the police arrested Avery for having a gun while on probation, and the county Sheriff announced in a press conference that they knew Teresa Halbach had been murdered in the Avery Salvage Yard. The police also claimed to have found a bullet in Avery's garage.

On November 15th, Prosecutor Ken Kratz

officially charged Avery with first-degree intentional homicide, mutilation of a corpse, and possession of a firearm by a felon. Kratz also told the press that Avery's blood was found inside Halbach's RAV4 and that he was also the last person to see her alive.

Avery would plead not guilty to the charges of murder.

After the murder, different stories were revealed about the case, such as a report that Halbach didn't like going to the Avery residence because he would always come on to her. The last time she was there, he answered the door wearing only a towel. One of her best friends, Gina Haring, said Teresa told her that Avery creeped her out and she thought he always looked at her weirdly. Teresa didn't want to go back there, but this particular job was supposed to be with his neighbor and sister, Barb Tadych. So she went, thinking she wouldn't have to see Avery.

In January 2006, the FBI lab released their results after testing the burned bones found on the Avery property. They determined that the bones belonged to Teresa Halbach.

～

At that time, Avery had been in jail for three months after being charged with several felonies and was broke. Desperately needing a good lawyer, he settled his lawsuit against the county for only $400,000 and hired seasoned lawyers Dean Strang and Jerry Buting.

A few months later, in March 2006, detectives arrested Avery's nephew, sixteen-year-old Brendan Dassey, charging him with first-degree murder and sexual assault. They also accused him of helping to dispose of Halbach's body. The only evidence of Dassey's involvement came from several hours of the police interrogating him. The interrogation details would later come to the public's attention after Netflix released its documentary covering the case after Avery's conviction. The controversial interrogation centered around Dassey's inability to handle himself alone with detectives considering his very low IQ.

Suspicion also fell on Teresa's ex-boyfriend, Ryan Hillegas. Teresa dated Ryan for a few years, but they split just before she went missing. It was, in fact, Ryan, along with some of her other friends, who led the search party looking for the missing Teresa on November 5th. They also found Teresa's RAV4 on the Avery property and reported it to the police. Ryan's leading the search would later cause another controversy. Some people speculated that Ryan was somehow involved in her disappearance and that he should not have been involved in the search. Conspiracies also suggested that he might have known where the RAV4 was and that it was far too coincidental that he found the vehicle on the first day of their search.

The 2007 Trial

The trial was being recorded by the production company that was creating the documentary series titled *Making a Murderer* for Netflix. But it was not shown live. The public often overlooked the people who lived in the area.

In the preliminary trial held in January 2007, the charges of kidnapping and sexual assault against Avery were dropped. The judge also ruled about what evidence could be presented at the trial. The defense's case centered around their belief that police had planted evidence to try and frame Avery for the murder. They believed that Avery's $36 million lawsuit against them was the primary motive for the framing. If he were convicted of this murder, it would drastically reduce the amount of the payout to him, if not wholly eliminate it. At that time, Avery had not settled.

On January 31st, Judge Patrick Willis ruled that the defense could present the evidence of Avery's blood being left unattended, which supported their claim that the evidence could have been manipulated and even planted at the crime scene. Another critical decision was that the defense could bring up Avery's $36 million lawsuit against the same county and police for imprisoning him wrongly for rape in 2005. These were both parts of the defense's argument about why the police were trying to frame Avery for Halbach's murder.

Another key ruling for the defense came just three days before the trial began. The judge decided to let them test the blood sample that was supposed to have been collected by detectives from Halbach's car. The defense believed it was indeed Avery's blood, but it was taken from his 1995 case and planted in her car. They were looking for the preservative EDTA, which was put in the vials of blood samples that the police take to preserve the blood. If this chemical was in the blood sample taken from her car, it came from a previous blood sample from a different case.

The trial began on Monday, February 13, 2007. In the opening statement by the defense, they contended that the detectives planted the blood evidence in Halbach's car and declared outright that they could prove her burned remains had been burned somewhere else, not on Avery's property, and that they were later placed among Avery's ashes in his fire pit. Strang also mentioned that police had searched the garage several times during the investigation and had not found a bullet. Then all of a sudden, one appeared months later.

Chapter 3
Brendan Dassey

B rendan Dassey was the sixteen-year-old nephew of Steven Avery, who lived in the next-door trailer. It was a complete surprise to not only the Avery family but everyone in the community as to why he was suddenly arrested as an accessory to the murder of Teresa Halbach. Even the Avery defense team had no idea what evidence the police had against him or how it would affect the trial.

On day three of the trial, defense attorney Strang filed for a mistrial claiming that Dassey's testimony would amount to a confession of a crime and that prosecutors should have informed him about Dassey's confessions. Prosecutor Kratz contended that the defense team had the complete transcripts of Dassey's interrogation by police months before the trial. Kratz also decided to prosecute Dassey in a separate test on April 16th. Dassey was also being charged with the murder and rape of Teresa Halbach.

Dassey was born on October 19, 1989, in Manitowoc County, Wisconsin, to Peter and Barb Dassey and had three older brothers and a half-brother. His parents separated only months after his birth, and he would go live with his mother in a trailer on the Avery Salvage Yard property, which sat next to Steven Avery's trailer.

Brendan had a learning disability in school. He had an extremely low IQ and struggled considerably in high school, so his mother put him in special education classes. Brendan was regularly teased and bullied at school, and other than trying to fight back against the bullies, he showed no criminal behavior inside or outside of school.

Dassey was known to love professional wrestling and frequently watched WWE shows on television. He was considered shy, an introvert, and had very low self-esteem. He would often spend time alone with animals and loved people's pets.

Detectives decided to interrogate Brendan after Steven Avery used him as his alibi for the day Teresa Halbach went missing. Initially, they just wanted to see if Dassey was really at home and could stand up to testimony in court. They interviewed Brendan four times over two days without any parent or guardian in the room.

Their interviewing technique of Brendan Dassey would end up being a significant issue with his testimony. He was slow and had nobody with him over all the hours that professional detectives were asking him questions. Detectives claimed they had Brendan's and his mother's permission to question him at the police station. After several hours of using pressured techniques and making false promises, Brendan confessed to the murder and rape of Teresa Halbach.

∼

Brendan's trial started on April 16, 2007, and only lasted a few days. Nine days later, he was convicted of first-degree murder, sexual assault, and the mutilation of a dead body. He was sentenced to life imprisonment and sent to the Columbia Correctional Institute in Wisconsin. He appealed his conviction in 2010, but the judge wouldn't even hear the appeal. His lawyers went to the Supreme Court in 2013, but they, too, wouldn't hear the case. Both trials had ended, and both Steven Avery and Brendan Dassey were convicted and sent away to prison for life.

After both tried to appeal their cases and were rejected, it looked like it was all over for them. At least until December 2015, when the production company making a docuseries about Avery's original wrongful conviction case had finished their project and sold it to the new streaming television service, Netflix.

This series would not only put Netflix on the map but also lead them to become the largest online streaming service. It also created a storm of controversy all over the country on television and online. But would it change things?

~

Later in August 2016, Dassey's conviction was overturned by a federal court judge stating that police coerced Dassey to get a confession out of him that was unconstitutional. On November 16th of that same year, Dassey was ordered to be released within 90 days if the current District Attorney did not charge and retry him. The next day, prosecutors filed an appeal, and the appeals court blocked the release of Dassey until the appeal was heard. In December 2017, a panel of seven courts of appeal judges listened to the case and, by a vote of four to three, affirmed Dassey's conviction. Today, he remains in prison. Later, the Supreme Court refused to hear his case.

Chapter 4
Making a Murderer Documentary

Between 2005 and 2015, Laura Ricciardi and Moira Demos wrote and filmed the first season of *Making a Murderer*, which covered the life of Steven Avery from his childhood through the eighteen years he was wrongfully imprisoned in 1985 and then to his conviction for the murder of Teresa Halbach.

The ten-episode series began to air on Netflix on December 18, 2015. This series created so much controversy over both of the trials of Steven Avery that a petition was started asking the White House to release Avery on the Halbach murder conviction. The petition gathered over 500,000 signatures. The *Making a Murderer* series was compared to other acclaimed series, such as HBO's *The Jinx,* and would receive four Emmy Awards.

Many aspects shown in each episode became the topic that the public widely talked about, including everyone involved in the trial. The case, originally thought to be over, was now open again, and the prosecutors and defense attorneys now had to answer the questions from viewers instead of journalists from newspapers and television.

Ken Kratz and the rest of his prosecution team stated that the series was one-sided and that they left out some key evidence. They claimed that the series was emotionally manipulative to the audience. Kratz also claimed that the series would make him out to be evil and purposely out to get Avery out of hate, which was not true.

Kratz did an interview with the national magazine *People,* where he listed out the evidence that he thought the series left out on purpose to make the viewers feel sorry for Avery and believe that police framed him. He also claimed that the filmmakers never interviewed or asked him to be part of the series, making it one-sided. Later, the filmmakers responded with proof of contacting

Kratz's office several times, trying to get him to talk on the record for the series, but he refused.

Kratz said that the series never mentioned that Avery used a fake name when asking for Halbach to come to his trailer and take photos of a van he had for sale. He claimed Avery did this because he figured if she knew it was Avery who wanted her to come out to the property, she probably wouldn't show up.

Kratz claimed another thing the series failed to mention was that Avery had called Halbach's cell phone three times on the day she went missing. He also said that Halbach's cell phone, camera, and PDA were all found near Avery's trailer and that they had found Avery's DNA on her RAV4 hood latch. Also, the bullet they found in his garage was fired from Avery's rifle.

Kratz's criticism was followed by Manitowoc County Sheriff Robert Hermann when he told *The Herald Times* that the series was skewed and not objective at all like a documentary was supposed to be. Yet, later in the interview, he admitted to never having watched even one episode of the series.

Dean Strang, one of Avery's defense attorneys, believed that the series did a great job of showing the critical elements of the case. He said that in a problem that was six weeks long, there would probably be over 240 hours recorded, so not everything could be shown in the series. It would be way too long, and people watching would lose interest and probably stop watching.

When I watched the series, I found the most crucial part to be the covering of Brendan Dassey's interrogation. His interrogation would probably become the most widely contested segment on almost any show covering the cases. It was controversial in many ways. Dassey's supporters claimed that it was unconstitutional for a seventeen-year-old boy with a low IQ to be interviewed by seasoned detectives for several hours alone. He was impressionable and unable to handle the interview. The big question was, How could there not have been a parent, guardian, or lawyer in the interrogation room with him?

The other controversial element surrounding the Dassey interview was his supposed confession of what happened that night when Teresa Halbach went missing. In many of the scenes aired in the series, the detectives would feed answers to Dassey. When Dassey answered a question or told them something happened that was wrong, they would then tell him the correct answer.

Whatever side you take on this case, there is no disputing that Dassey did not have counsel with him, and the detectives did coerce him into saying things during the interviews.

Part Two

THE PROSECUTION

Chapter 5
Interview with Ken Kratz

K en Kratz was the District Attorney of Calumet County, Wisconsin, during the Steven Avery and Brendan Dassey trials for the murder and sexual assault of Teresa Halbach in 2007. Kratz was thrown into the spotlight after the release of the *Making a Murderer* series, where he was portrayed as the "bad guy." The series only showed him in parts where he was saying bad things about both defendants, and the series never interviewed him to try and find out where he was coming from throughout the trial.

To make matters worse and to show Kratz as an even more evil and corrupt prosecutor, the series covered a sexual scandal he was involved in during 2010, after which he resigned from his job in October of that year. Kratz's law license was also suspended for four months in 2014. The series presented the case even though it had nothing to do with either of the Avery or Dassey cases. A 26-year-old preschool teacher, Stephanie Van Groll, filed a complaint with him about her ex-boyfriend, who had nearly choked her to death. Kratz was the prosecutor of cases like this and a veteran chair of the Wisconsin Crime Victim's Rights Board. He reprimanded judges, prosecutors, and police officers who mistreated victims of crimes and domestic abuse.

After he met with Van Groll, she claimed that Kratz had sent her over thirty texts in three days, which were sexual. Some of the texts released to the media were, "Are you the kind of girl that likes secret contact with an older married elected DA? The riskier, the better." Kratz also wrote things suggesting having more of an affair, "I would not expect you to be the other woman. I would want you to be so hot and treat me so well that you'd be THE woman! R U that good?" Van Groll claimed that Kratz said he would drop all charges against her ex-boyfriend if she didn't have an affair with him.

During the series, they showed him in his office responding to the claims about his sexual harassment of Van Groll. He responded with only concern about how publishing his texts to her would unfairly embarrass him personally and professionally. He did not deny any of the claims. On camera, he said, "This is a non-news story; I'm worried about it because of my reputational interests." His reaction caused the loudest backlash toward Kratz, making it easy for people to hate him.

Not only was Kratz removed from the prosecution case of the assault charges against Van Groll's ex-boyfriend, but he was removed from the victim's crime board, and his wife filed for divorce in December of that same year. Van Groll would respond in anger to the *Associated Press* afterward, saying, "They slapped him on the wrist and told him not to do it again. If it were anybody else that did something like this, they'd lose their job."

The series also showed other instances when Kratz had texted further women he met while working as a prosecutor on their cases. During an investigation of Kratz, the Wisconsin Department of Justice made a one hundred and forty-three-page report, and the series exposed the details of it. *Newsweek* obtained documents from that investigation that included allegations of Kratz leaving a woman $75 after his threats scared her into performing oral sex on him. The report also talked about Kratz trying to pick up a girl from *Craigslist* by boasting about being the man who prosecuted Steven Avery. Another piece discussed a woman shoplifter whom Kratz told he would not put in jail if she had sex with him. Even though there were several reports of Kratz behaving in this way, the DOJ decided not to press charges. Their decision infuriated the viewers against Kratz.

In February 2017, Ken Kratz wrote a book covering the Avery case and trial, which he released. So I had an opportunity to sit down with him on two occasions and interview him about the book. This interview took place in October 2018.

Q. Why do you think there's such a backlash towards you?

A. That's a great question, Alan. From my perspective, it's just a matter of math. Forty million people watched *Making a Murderer*. At the time, it was the largest and most watched streaming entertainment event of all time. It's only been eclipsed by the Netflix show *Birdbox*. That's the most people that had ever watched something. Certainly, the filmmakers never expected that kind of response. Netflix never expected that kind of response.

But, when you have forty million people being shown one side of a case, and not even the side, Alan, that was shown to the jury. In other words, *Making a Murderer* presented an alternate version of the evidence, an alternative version of the facts. I've been highly critical that the filmmakers omitted very important evidence that showed Steven Avery was guilty of this crime. But when you have forty million people being told that cops, as an example, planted evidence, or that there was a purple topped tube of blood in the clerk's office and having one of the lawyers recorded on the T.V. show saying, "That's what proves that they took that blood and that they planted evidence," it's awfully hard to overcome that kind of narrative. The truth, of course, Alan, is the famous purple-topped tube that attorney Jerry Buting refers to had a hole in the top of it, and of course, you recall, I'm sure that proved, if you will, that the cops tampered with the vile of blood and the cops planted evidence and went a long way towards Sergeant Colborn and Lieutenant Lenk being really pointedly criticized for not only the investigation but that the takeaway conclusion was that they chose to set up an innocent man for murder and to go to prison.

The question I would ask you, Alan, is what happens when it becomes proven that the purple-topped tube was not sketchy at all? What happens when Jerry Buting, as an example, gets a written, sworn statement from a nurse named Marlene Kranitz that says, "I'm the one who put the hole in the purple-topped tube." That's how blood gets into a vacutainer. A purple-topped tube. That makes sense.

So, Jerry Buting got that written statement before the trial, Alan. He had that information before the trial. He knew that the tube wasn't tampered with. He knew that evidence and that the blood inside of it was not used to plant, not any blood. In fact, we had disproved that at trial by the FBI. They proved that there was no preservative, called EDTA, in the blood stains inside the RAV4, yet the purple-topped tube was chock-full of EDTA, which scientifically proved that.

But beyond that, the fact that the lawyers knew that the cops didn't plant any evidence, the fact that the filmmakers knew that these two honest, really impeccably seasoned officers, with no history of any misconduct, with no history of any discipline. You made 40 million people believe that they were crooks. And that these guys were willing to frame an innocent man. The result, of course, is that maybe your listeners don't even know that Sergeant Colborn was completely trashed by worldwide people. Every day he got death threats, and he still does to this day. Every day he was called crooked. Every day his reputation was tarnished more and more and more publicly.

Even after *Making a Murderer's* release, even after people like Jerry Buting, Laura Ricciardi, and Moira Demos for the film. Even though they knew it was a lie, they continued perpetuating that myth. They continued to push their narrative that the cops planted evidence to get these guys convicted. Well, when it's proven beyond all doubt that that didn't happen. When it's proven beyond all doubt that these filmmakers lied and that they made up these things for a documentary – if they can call it that. They did things like splicing testimony into court exchanges to fool the audience into thinking something else was said. These are the kinds of editing techniques that, up until 2015, would never have been sanctioned or never been unscrutinized, I guess, by the documentary film industry or anybody else that cares about this kind of thing.

Not only were these filmmakers not taken to task for that, Alan, and not only were these filmmakers not criticized for what's been proven to be splicing or what's been proven to be presenting a false narrative, but they were given four Emmy Awards for this, including one for editing. Well, when that happens, you're at the receiving end of this vitriol. You're at the receiving end of these lies that make the villains cast in *Making a Murderer* seem like crooks when the prosecution and law enforcement seem like they targeted an innocent man. When 40 million people believe that, that's the case.

Then you have the former prosecutor, who

by that time had already been resoundingly criticized when he puts out a book, and there's this concerted effort to give it one-star reviews on Amazon, so nobody reads the book. They pan it, they trash it, and all these misconceptions and mistruths are allowed to perpetuate. It gets very frustrating.

So, when I present things like unedited clips, or when I present things too, like, here's what the jury got to see, I don't really want to try and convince anybody that's entrenched in what they think. But I do want them to know that there's another side. There's a whole side that you haven't seen. In fact, important to some of your listeners, it was the version of the evidence that the jury got to see. It wasn't edited. It wasn't created for television. It was presented at trial – in both trials – which resulted in both of these guys getting convicted of first-degree intentional homicide.

So, hopefully, somebody that's in your audience will pause and say, "Well, that makes sense." If we were fooled, if 40 million people were fooled by these filmmakers, we'd probably want to be told that. It's okay that we're shown how we were fooled. But what happens, Alan, and you may know this, people get so defensive when they have already taken a position, when they've already publicly announced that "We support Steven Avery" or "We support the version that was presented to us in this ten-hour docuseries." It's hard thereafter to admit that, well, wait for a second. We were fooled. We were told things that never happened. They led us down this path. And you've got to raise your hand and say, "I'm guilty. I thought Ken Kratz was a creeper, or a jerk, or a person that didn't have this kind of evidence."

More important were the two cops that were involved. When you come away thinking that they were crooked or sketchy or any of that kind of stuff. And it was only because it was exactly what the filmmakers wanted you to see. These are people that have had a very real impact on this T.V. show. It's ruined the lives of at least those two cops. Mine? I lost my law firm directly because of *Making a Murderer*.

All of these consequences on the people that were involved in the case fourteen years ago, which at the time was described as a highly competent and very well-litigated major case in the United States. But that script has obviously been flipped since 2015.

My job is to put things out there to show

there is another side. People, please take a look at this other side before you jump to too many conclusions and, at the very least, give people a chance to make a decision for themselves on what really happened.

Q. Looking over your new book reviews – and there are already hundreds of terrible reviews – most of them were reviewing you as a person and not the content of the book.

A. No. Seventy-nine of those one-star reviews came out before the book was even out or before they could have even read the book. Amazon, by the way, we contacted them and knew there were fake reviews. But they said they don't take off fake reviews just because they're trying to impact sales. That aside, we're not going to get political, but there's a woman named Hilary Clinton that wrote a book, and on Amazon, the same thing happened to her with all the one-star reviews. Check this for yourself; all the one-star reviews she had, Amazon removed. They said this couldn't be real because nobody could have read the book. Suddenly, their position about cleaning up fake reviews is applied to somebody like Mrs.

Clinton. But when it's very clear, in fact, they admitted they know that these are fake reviews to pan my book, they refused to address that issue on their own site.

The people that have read the book believe it's easy to read, it's well written, it's got a lot of pictures, it's got a lot of evidence, it's very clear step-by-step to show you what the jury saw, and then I invite people to decide for themselves. In fact, you may recall that in the first chapter, I said not to believe a word I said. All evidence is there, and I'm asking you to consider it yourselves.

Q. We are currently in a conspiracy climate here in America, and we see it a lot in our politics, so there are many people out there right now that picture you with the black hat on and believe that you were in on the conspiracy to get an innocent man convicted. How are you going to get people away from that kind of thinking?

A. So, let me ask a couple of obvious questions. Who made them think that? It wasn't at the time of the trial. At the time of the trial, these guys were guilty. All the people from Wisconsin who got to watch this case—it was on wall-to-wall coverage for this seven-week trial—and Wisconsin residents were convinced after watching it and all of the evidence that the jury in both cases made the correct decision.

Every court that looked at the appeal, whether it was a circuit court or an appeals court, whether it was a state court or federal court, every court at every stage has upheld the conviction. So, you've got to ask yourself, Alan, what don't we know? What haven't we been shown? Somebody thinks that these guys are guilty. The juries, the court, the prosecution, everybody who sat through the trial, so what haven't we been shown? That's my point, Alan.

If there are that many people contemporaneous to when it happened, whereas at the time that this was presented, there was an almost universal belief that justice had been done, and it was only this film that, more than ten years after the fact, threw shade on this particular case because of the agenda of the filmmakers, isn't that something that you want to look in more.

Q. But how are you going to get over it?

A. Yes, how am I going to get over it? How am I going to get over the negative attachment, the ad hominem attacks on me? But Kratz, he did this. He did that. We can't believe anything he says despite it being a presentation of the evidence.

It's not going to be from me, Alan. I can't repair my reputation. I can't tell people, you know, shake my fist at the sky and say, "But you haven't read everything; you don't know this." That's not going to do any good. It's going to take people like you. It's going to take people like your listeners. It's going to take a tipping point to occur where the Netflix viewers finally realize, "Hey, something screwy happened; something terrible happened to these cops."

They really were unfairly impacted. Their whole lives were unfairly impacted because of this. This shouldn't happen and get people to take a fresh look at it and look at the evidence. Not through the eyes of 'We think Ken Kratz is horrible or deserves to be killed,' which is most of the things that you see on the internet.

But I'll tell Alan; I'm up against it. Nobody wants to believe they're fooled. Nobody wants to believe my side of the story. Everyone likes to think that this poor kid Brendan Dassey should get out. You know he's got big hitters like Kim Kardashian. and others who have come out publicly supporting him. I've got what, eight followers on Twitter? Against Kardashian with sixty-two million. It's going to get drowned out and not even heard. It's going to take somebody other than me. In fact, it's going to take a lot of somebodies other than me to at least say, "Take a look at the other side before you sign a petition."

Q. So, do you think that the people who made this documentary had it in their minds to do this?

A. When the filmmakers—two film students at the time from Columbia University—asked Dean Strang and Jerry Buting if they could join the team, if they could embed themselves with the defense team and be able to shoot things in real-time or strategy sessions, or when they found things out that they could report them, all of their objectivity was taken from them. They had no objectivity. They became an investigative arm of the defense team.

I said that before the case concluded. If you're going to be an investigative arm of the defense, then we're entitled to see your footage. We'd like to see what it is that you've been sharing with Mr. Strang and Mr. Buting from things that you've individually found out. As an example, it's well known that the two filmmakers knew of the existence of this vial of blood in the Clerk of the Court's office in the Summer of 2006. Yet the state wasn't told about it by the defense and certainly not by the filmmakers until December of 2006.

That's five months that they all knew about this vial of blood and didn't tell us. Why? Because they didn't want us to be able to test it. They didn't want us to be able to disprove that this was not the blood that was used. Strang and Buting rolled the dice and hoped that that late disclosure would make it impossible for us to send the evidence in and have it tested in time. They were almost right.

But, what most of your listeners are not aware of is that the FBI, in February 2007, closed their lab for three weeks to handle one case. The one case that the FBI handled was the Avery case. The FBI closed the lab to develop a protocol for the testing of EDTA, which was a preservative found there. You may recall back to the O.J. Simpson case; that was the first time the EDTA concept was brought up as there was a planting defense. You could look at the blood, the blood that was actually recovered, and say, "Does it have EDTA in it?" It's a preservative that's in every purple-topped tube, so if you have blood from any of those tubes, you're going to find EDTA. So, when it's not there, it is a powerful piece of evidence. Because the protocol hadn't been developed correctly enough or carefully enough after the O.J. case, the results were not allowed into evidence, and so it didn't work. What happened in the interim? What happened between the O.J. case and the Avery case was that the crime lab in the FBI was developing a protocol on how do you test for EDTA. So, that entire three-week time period, there was a head of the lab at that time, and his name was Mark LeBeau, and he developed the protocol for testing the EDTA in the entire lab.

In fact, they were able to find that the blood discovered, in fact, had no EDTA in it. And as I said before, the vial was chock full of it, and we were able to present that at trial. We got the results maybe one or two days before we were going to rest our case, and I presented that evidence. So the jury got to hear that this planting nonsense never happened. This was made up by the defense. And, of course, the jury heard that. And we blew the defense out of the water just with that evidence.

It goes well beyond that that after the fact, the filmmakers again knew that it was false information and presented it anyway. That's the kind of thing that I don't know if I was watching a docudrama and deciding if I should believe this. All of the places that they misrepresented. All the places that they spliced in words that were never there in real life. When they splice in an answer that famously, don't you think it's suspicious when Andy Colborn has been questioned by Dean Strang about the license plates when the license plates were called in? He was asked, "Don't you think that looks suspicious?" and he admits, "Yes, it looks suspicious." Then the music comes in. What your listeners, I'm sure, don't know, Alan is the "Yes" answer never happened in real life. In real life, I objected to the question. The court never allowed that question to be answered. But, in *Making a Murderer*, you see him answering, "Yes." You see him saying, "Yes, it was suspicious." Well, where does that come from, Alan? Where it comes from is the answer is harvested from another part of the interview in the trial, and it's spliced in as if that was really his answer. Well, what the hell is that, Alan? What documentary, if you can call it that, gets away with that? What documentary splices in an answer that never happened in real life? Then when they're called on it, they say, "We never said that it was true. We said that this was just for entertainment purposes." That certainly changes things, doesn't it?

Q. It sort of sounds like Alex Jones.

A. Well, it's so deceptive not to at least tell these people that this never happened, by the way, in real life. What we're showing you is made up for T.V. What we're showing you—this is the sad part—is made up to make this man look sketchy. To make this cop, who's a good honest cop who couldn't lie about anything, we spliced it in here to make him look guilty. The impact that it has on him later, well, to hell with that. We don't care that forever he's going to be known as a crooked cop. We got good ratings. Because we spliced that in, and it was very dramatic. We became the biggest show of all time.

Now, after the fact, now that we know and Netflix knows it's a lie, Netflix knows that they spliced that in; how come that hasn't been changed, Alan? How come that hasn't been fixed? How come they haven't gone back and either taken this out of the documentary genre? Or why haven't they issued a retraction or an apology? Or what's happened as a result of their not even carelessness, their intentional misrepresentation?

You know, I watched *Game of Thrones*, and there was a coffee cup left in a scene, and by the time I watched it again, it had already been removed. Netflix has had four years. Why the hell isn't this fixed? You know that it's a lie. Keep perpetrating it, and when somebody like Andy Colborn sues you for defamation. And he says "that you are intentionally making me look sketchy for your ratings, and to my detriment," when he sues you, and you've got the guts to act surprised about that. You've got the guts to say we can't be sued for defamation because we've got all kinds of protection.

Is there a line that needs to be drawn to be called a documentary? How about the line is you don't get to splice things in to make it look like something happened that didn't really happen? That seems like an easy line to draw, and that's where I think we should start.

Q. One of the biggest things that people who watched the series was Brendan Dassey's confession. The claim is that he had an intellectual disability and that he should have never been interviewed alone, and even if he didn't request to have someone else in the interrogation room with him, there still should have been someone put in the room by the police. What are your thoughts on that?

A. They asked his mom, Alan.

Q. Yes, that's true. But so...

A. This is a serious question.

Q. I know.

A. If his mom sat through that March first interview, let's say she sat through the entire interview, would that have alleviated the concerns of all of the people who are clamoring that there should have been a lawyer or parent present?

Well, you'd think the answer would be yes, right? That would be good enough. So, when Barb, the mother of Brendan Dassey, at Brendan's post-conviction hearing, was asked, "Well, weren't you invited to sit through every one of these interviews?" When Barb testified under oath, "Yes, yes, I was asked to sit through them all by the cops. I was the one who rejected that. I was the one who said to interview him alone; I don't want to be in there while he's being interviewed."

Well, isn't that what they wanted? To at least give the parent an option to sit through, which Barb was given. How many people know that, Alan? How many people know that Barb herself chose not to sit through those interviews? Of the six times he's interviewed, five of the times, I believe, requested to, or invited to, sit through. One of the other times, a lawyer was invited to sit through. So, the fact that that didn't happen by his own lawyer or by his own parent, I'm not sure how the state of Wisconsin is criticized for this kid making a statement.

Here's the other important thing, though. On March 1st, Brendan Dassey was not a suspect. This was a witness interview like any other child interview. If you've ever seen those being conducted? The whole beginning of that kind of child witness is when a child has seen something that is disturbing, traumatizing, or hard to describe. Certain things are said to kids to get them to talk. It's called "rapport-building," at least in the protocol for interviewing child witnesses. But, in rapport-building, here are the things you say to them, "It's okay; we already know what happened." You say to kids at the rapport-building start of the interview, "Your mom encouraged you to be honest. We hope that you are going to be honest with us. I know what you've seen is traumatic. You might have to use bad words or language, but we've heard it all before." Those are the kind of assurances made to them.

So, at 11:45 in the morning, about forty-five minutes after the interview started, Brendan makes his first admission. For the first time, Brendan moves from a witness to a traumatized witness, if not a victim himself of what happened, to a suspect. He places himself there. He admits that he raped Teresa Halbach. So, up until that time, cops had no idea that Brendan Dassey himself was involved.

How do we know that? We know because I

set up that interview. I talked to the cops before that interview. I told the cops to make sure that you're in a soft room and it's gentle in there. And it's recorded. And it's going to be a child witness interview that someday might have to be used. What he saw was probably horrific, whether it was on the fire or in the garage, or anywhere else.

So, the fact that there's this perception out there that the cops wanted him to say just what they wanted to hear, well, that's foolish because the cops had no idea what was going to come out of his mouth. The cops had no idea that he was involved. They were looking for what he had seen to implicate Steven Avery. Tell us the truth about what you saw, and only the truth because that's the only thing that's going to help us. When he admitted that he himself was involved in the crime, what did you expect to have happened?

Well, the cops then said, "Well, tell us all about that?" The cops then changed, as you'll see on a new series of videos that I posted on the Brendan Dassey statements, the March 1st statement, unedited. It's out there for people to make up their own minds. But, on the unedited version, you'll see the change in Agent

Fassbender. For example, when Brendan says, "Here's what happened. Here's what I saw," the next question, just like any other good interview, is an open-ended, "Well, tell me everything about that?"

So Brendan does that, Alan. Brendan gives a narrative version about what happened. About the rape, about the murder. Almost completely narrative in his own words. So, assume that is in existence and shown to the jury, and Brendan's jury convicts him because they see him in his own words telling what happened.

What happens, though, Alan is that nobody is ever shown that. Nobody is ever shown that part of his statement, that part of his admission. Well, you may say, well, the entire Brendan Dassey confession is on *YouTube*, let's say, or the internet. You can find all four hours of the interview, and you can sit through four hours of him being questioned, and you can satisfy yourself, okay, now I have seen the whole confession.

Here's the problem, Alan, whoever put Brendan Dassey's on, a supporter of Brendan Dassey, and had 500,000 people watch it. Five hundred thousand people watched Brendan's complete interview and then sat back and said now we're convinced that we saw the whole confession. Ken, you're wrong; he didn't admit to being involved in rape or murder. How can you say that? So, my second video that I post and that's on *YouTube* and that I invite people to look at is the *YouTube* Brendan Dassey confession. The *YouTube* version, the official version, if you will. Go and watch the whole thing. They're invited to do and have your viewers looking at that video, and at 11:55 a.m., when his admission, remember his free narrative, what he did, begins until 12:24 p.m. That's about thirty minutes later. That thirty minutes of Brendan's confession is removed. It's completely edited out of the official version that 500,000 people watched online. My second video shows you.

Why would they remove all of his admission? Who would remove all of Brendan Dassey's confession about the rape, the murder, and the free narrative that's not in response to a leading question? That's not fed to him. It's a free narrative about what happened. Why wouldn't that be on the official confession? The answer should be obvious. That somebody does not want you to see that Brendan actually confessed.

Q. Both Avery and Dassey were tried separately and convicted separately.

A. Yes.

Q. In both cases, there's a completely different storyline on how the murders happened. A lot of what Brendan Dassey said couldn't have happened or probably didn't happen. For example, there was no blood or DNA found in Avery's bedroom, where they were supposed to have been tied to his bed and raped by both of them and then knifed to death, according to Dassey.

A. Let me stop you, Alan because you got to unpack like four things. There are four things that you mentioned here, four complaints, and you've got to take them one at a time here. Let's first talk about there being no Brendan in the bedroom. The biggest complaint that you see online now is that nothing puts Brendan in that room, and until there's some physical DNA, I'm not going to believe his confession.

Tell that to millions of rape victims that you needed some kind of physical evidence to prove that rape happened. I want these "Me Too" supporters to go online and say we're not going to believe a rape happened unless there's physical DNA evidence to prove it. The question is, what DNA would you expect to find? What would you expect to find from Brendan Dassey in that room? Brendan Dassey was interviewed and asked if he knew what the term ejaculate meant, and he did. They asked him if he ejaculated during the rape, and he said no, I did not. The fact is that if you talked to any CSI person, he wouldn't expect to find any of Brendan's DNA there. That's exactly what they found. None of his DNA was there. So, what does that mean there? Well, not very much.

Q. What about Teresa Halbach? Why wouldn't her DNA be there? If they had really raped her and then sliced her to death using a knife to her stomach, wouldn't there have been a lot of blood there?

A. The only witness that we had that was talking about what happened in that room was Brendan Dassey. Steven Avery is not telling you what happened. Steven Avery, by the way, had cleaned that room for four days before the cops got there. The day after Teresa Halbach is missing and the day after Teresa Halbach, we learn now, is killed, Steven Avery is shampooing the carpets in his trailer.

Now, you may not think that's a coincidence, you may not think that is something that would raise an eyebrow or two, but when he talks to his girlfriend Jody on the phone that week, he talks about Rug Doctoring all the carpets and rugs in his trailer. And by the way, Steven Avery lives in filth and squalor; you've seen the photos of his garage. The fact that he's scrubbing everything with bleach in his trailer, again, I don't mean to be suspicious, but it's something that you may want to look at. That completely falls on deaf ears, Alan. Nobody says, "I know he had four days to clean up. I know he admitted to shampooing the rugs, and I know that he knows that bleach kills DNA because he learned that the first time around. I know that he used a lot of bleach and paint thinner in the garage."

It splashed up on Brendan's jeans. We have the bleach-stained jeans that Brendan turned over, saying that these are the ones that, when we were cleaning things up, got splashed on. By the way, who says that's not physical evidence? Is there any physical evidence that corroborates what Brendan says? Well, there's his bleach-stained jeans which seem to be physical evidence.

How about the rivets from the Daisy Fuentes jeans that Teresa Halbach wore and when Brendan Dassey said after they carried her out to the garage after they took her clothes off, they took all of those clothes and put them on the fire pit. Brendan Dassey said, "I put those clothes on the fire." So, when they find the rivets to the jeans she was wearing that day, why isn't that physical evidence that they found that day? Why is everybody screaming that there's nothing that corroborates what Brendan said?

When Brendan says that uncle Steve went under the hood of the trunk, and later after Brendan said that they swabbed the hood latch and they found Steven's under the hood, which isn't accessible from the outside of the car, why isn't that shown on *Making a Murderer*?

Why isn't Teresa's phone, PDA, and camera that's burned up in Steven Avery's own personal burn barrel, those are electronics of Teresa's that are found in Avery's own burn barrel and were shown he was witnessed burning the afternoon of the thirty-first, which you may think is a coincidence. Because that evidence was shown to the jury, and all of her electronics were there in his house, why isn't *Making a Murderer* tell you that? Why doesn't *Making a Murderer* say, "Wait for a second; there's no explanation for this." Steven can't explain it.

The planting theory certainly can't explain all of these burned electronics in this place that only Steven Avery has access to. But why didn't they show the things that would prove him guilty? The answer is clear. It didn't fit their narrative, and it didn't fit poor Steven Avery has been attacked again. I shift topics, but these are so important that poor people just don't do very well. Steven Avery paid $240,000 to the two best lawyers in Wisconsin. Are you going to tell me that this was a poor person? Are you going to tell me that the defense that they put on was only something that poor people were able to afford? Are you kidding me? I've never heard of a lawyer taking two hundred and forty grand for a murder case for a person who wasn't a CEO.

Q. What are your thoughts about that current inmate, Joseph Evans Jr., who is now confessing to the Halbach murder?

A. Well, Kathleen Zellner puts this fake offer out there: 100 Grand for anybody who gives information that leads to the conviction of the real killer. By the way, Alan, there's only one person who could collect that, and that was me. Right, I'm the one who has presented the evidence that convicted her killer, so if she wants to write me a check, I'm certainly available for that. But that fake offer to invite these kooks to come forward to try and collect this thing is exactly what happened. Predictable. Foreseeable. It's exactly what happened. You get some murderer who clearly said, "I'm coming forward to collect this $100,000." So, whatever he says in about eight seconds, you can prove that he couldn't have possibly even been there that day. So, that goes under the category of you get what you asked for.

Q. How do you want people to find you, your book, or interact with you? Civilly.

A. I'm not sure I do, Alan.

Q. Oh?

A. I don't mean to be rude, but I put everything I had in my book, and I would ask that if they are willing to buy that, they can. I'm on Twitter, I guess, unfortunately, but it's a place where people can access me directly. I'm willing if people are polite and they have a question, to answer them one on one. I've been doing that with dozens of people right now. I'm happy to do that as long as you're polite and not attacking me or my family as part of your comments. The *YouTube* videos are available, and the book will be available on Amazon and most bookstores.

Listen to the full interview with Ken Kratz on my website:

https://www.alanrwarren.com/
hom-podcast-episodes/
episode/c745f569/ken-kratz-
new-inmate-confession

Chapter 6
Interview with Michael Griesbach

I first met Michael Griesbach well before all of the *Making a Murderer* drama started in late 2015. A year before the series was released, Griesbach wrote a book called *The Innocent Killer: A*

Story of a Wrongful Conviction and its Astonishing Aftermath, released in 2014. The book's premise was great, about a man who was wrongfully convicted of rape and assault and spent eighteen years in prison. Then, his case was overturned after DNA evidence came forward to prove his innocence.

There are several stories like this and books about this kind of thing happening in our justice system, but this case had an interesting twist that I had never encountered before. After Avery was released from prison, he sued Wisconsin for wrongful imprisonment. Still, he committed another rape during that time, only this time it resulted in the victim being murdered.

Even stranger was that when Avery was first released and began his lawsuit, he started to do media appearances about what happened to him. One of those appearances was on CNN's popular crime show, *Nancy Grace*. Just after that appearance, a warrant went out for his arrest, and he was on the run for the murder of Teresa Halbach.

What was even more amazing was that before he was even arrested, he made another appearance on the *Nancy Grace* show to try and explain how he had nothing to do with the

Halbach murder. And that law enforcement was trying to frame him for the murder so that they could get out of the lawsuit or at least have the settlement amount reduced from the $36 million that he was asking for to something far less, which eventually was settled at $400,000.

Michael Griesbach had been a state prosecutor for eighteen years in Wisconsin. He wrote the book as he explained to try and get readers more informed about the inner workings of the criminal justice system and how lives can be deeply affected before, during, and after a murder trial. Remember that the *Making a Murderer* series had not been released at the time of my first interview with Griesbach. At that time, none of us even knew when the series would get completed and that it would end up being as popular as it was. Griesbach was shown a few times in the first couple of episodes of the series but was not a major player in the Halbach murder case.

Griesbach was a very likable guy who appeared very honest and trustworthy. In short, I liked him and enjoyed having him on the show. At this time, my performance was fairly new and only in smaller markets, so I was grateful that not only did he come on the show but that he was accommodating and patient throughout the interview. The first interview was in late 2014.

After the series was released in December 2015, and the big explosion of sudden interest caught on, Griesbach was one of the victims of the crazy backlash brought upon anybody who was part of the state of Wisconsin law enforcement. He started receiving an onslaught of death threats, verbal abuse on the internet, and many attacks on his first book.

Two years later, Griesbach released a second book, again taking on the Avery case, only this time it was focused on what people were not seeing or hearing about the case from the *Making a Murderer* series on Netflix. I was again fortunate enough for him to agree to be on the show, covering such a heated subject.

This book covers only the key topics discussed in both interviews, but links to the full interviews are included here if you want to hear them from beginning to end.

After both discussions, I remained in contact with Griesbach and have had a few talks with him, as well as had to fight off some online abuse for just having him on the show. I also should mention that Griesbach has gone on to be the lawyer handling the Sergeant Colborn lawsuit against Netflix and the filmmakers of *Making a Murderer,* which is mentioned in the Ken Kratz interview and this book.

Q. The last time we talked, which was last May, you had written the book *The Innocent Killer,* and it seemed to be that the purpose of your writing this book was to show the wrongful conviction of Steven Avery. I wanted to start the show by mentioning that because of all the feedback from the *Making a Murderer* series.

A. You know, that's exactly right. I never dreamed that this would become a contentious thing, at least from that side of the equation. People think that I'm somehow an anti-Steven Avery, pro-law enforcement. If anything, when I wrote the book, I was more concerned about how my colleagues in law enforcement, especially the District Attorney, would view me and my book because I would go against the grain. I was taking to task my predecessors: the former law enforcement, the former sheriff, and the former DA, in a case. Imagine saying this is a wrongful conviction in 1985; this is a horrible conviction. Essentially, an intentional or reckless sending away an innocent person for eighteen years.

Yes, I think the focus, in fact, about two-thirds of my book, was about that. I think the last third touched off on Teresa Halbach's murder. I did try to bring in the lessons from criminal justice, and I spoke about wrongful convictions. I spoke about prosecutor misconduct. But here we are. What a difference television makes.

Q. Yes, that's how I saw it. Your book left me thinking more about wrongful convictions and not so much about Teresa Halbach, which, I guess, is bad in a way but certainly not intentional. For me, the main focus of your book and interview was about the eighteen years Avery served in prison for something he didn't do. This was also before the *Making a Murderer* series came out too. How was it for you to continue to work with law enforcement in the county after you released that book?

A. I was surprised to some extent. Well, maybe not completely surprised. The police, for instance, especially the Manitowoc City Police Department, different officers in court would say, "Thanks a lot for writing that book and explaining what the police, the sheriff, and a handful of the sheriff's department, a different agency, and the former district attorney did because they appreciate it, you know."

Your listeners won't believe this, but most police actually want the bad apples to be out there. They wanted them to be held accountable because, like any profession, there are some bad apples among police and among prosecutors. I do think the vast majority of them would never do anything like what happened in the first Avery case. They're interested in trying to do their best to seek justice in the tough system. That's not to say that there isn't a special authority, especially with the police, that's unchecked when they're out in the streets. Although cameras, body cameras have really helped that a lot. So, is there a greater danger? I think there is, frankly, of what the bad apples can do in these positions. The same as, some prosecutors were probably given way too much power and discretion in the court system. But the bottom line is most police are not interested in doing that sort of thing. They are decent people. They are people's husbands and fathers who, right now, are not a real easy job, frankly kind of a dangerous job. When I wrote the book, they appreciated it.

Now the prosecutors have been a little standoffish, but not so much in my office. I'm friends with them, but prosecutors throughout the state, with the exception of just a few, have met me with a kind of cold silence. I don't think they liked that I suggested that a former prosecutor essentially, intentionally or recklessly, at the least, sent an innocent guy away to prison. We can be an arrogant lot. I'll confess that right here. It's an occupational hazard. Call a prosecutor on a mistake and say you did this, and you shouldn't have done that. If you want to watch somebody get defensive real quick, that's the way you do it.

Q. But you actually took this further. You took the evidence to Madison (the capital of Wisconsin) and tried to get something done to your predecessor. So, it wasn't like you just let it happen?

A. No. We got really troubled, myself and another DA, by what they did. We took it to the Wisconsin State Attorney's office for an independent review. She whitewashed the entire affair, and that's what I wrote in the book. That was the top Wisconsin law enforcement official at the time. That's not the AG now. When we took it there, she basically blamed it on tunnel vision and found no criminal or ethical misconduct on the part of the former sheriff and former DA, which frankly is nonsense in my view.

Q. What do you think all of the negative backlashes are all about? Was it the way that the *Making a Murderer* series portrayed you?

A. Well, I think that's a good chunk of it. *Making a Murderer* came in the context of a strong feeling throughout the country that, and I'm not saying anything that you and your listeners aren't fully aware of, but a strong distrust of our police, especially in urban areas with the police shootings that are very troubling and the racial stuff, which is very troubling.

There is a slew of recent cases, Appellant Court cases, especially in California and in New York, accompanied by media attention with *New York Times* opinions and prosecutor misconduct. Prosecutor arrogance and the prosecutor's failure to disclose what we call "exculpatory evidence," which is evidence that could help a defendant suggest maybe an innocent or maybe the defendant didn't do it. There have been too many incidents where they failed to turn the evidence over, and the reactions by the prosecutors on these cases and the U.S. Attorney's Office is sometimes the worst. It has been, "Ah, no big deal. We didn't mean to do that. We won't do it again."

So, that's the context of when this comes in. So, I get why people are upset. There is, though, in addition to that; that's just the context. But *Making a Murderer* itself, while it did some good things by bringing attention to the criminal justice system to a wide group of people who usually wouldn't care that much, also did a huge disservice, in my opinion, by presenting a one-sided agenda-driven version of what happened in this particular case in the county where I still work as a district attorney.

Q. I think the most shocking for viewers was the Brendan Dassey interrogations by the police, where he had no attorney or parent with him during the interviews, and it seemed they had set him up. But none of that is illegal or against the rules, is it? That is a legal way to interview someone, isn't it?

A. It is to a point. It's called the "Reid Technique" from some former cop or psychologist or something in Northern Illinois. It's used all across the country. That is troubling. My family and I watched the documentary together, and we were troubled by that. I had kind of heard portions of it, but I didn't realize just how aggressive the interrogation of Brendan Dassey, who is obviously emotionally, or at least intellectually, had some shortcomings. Some people would argue that he's got the equivalent of maybe a sixth grader in terms of recognizing what might happen after this.

Yeah, I completely, and in fact, I very much separate Brendan Dassey's case and the Steven Avery case as much as I can because they get integrated eventually. The courts are going to have to take a good look at that. That case is in federal court in Milwaukee, so I can't focus too much on it. But I can say that they really need to wrestle with that, and I'm sure they will figure out whether they crossed the line legally. Many people think that, and I don't know that I disagree. The courts are allowing too much of that kind of interrogation by police, where the goal is to break the person down and have them confess to a crime that the police are convinced the person did, as opposed to finding out the truth.

The two police officers, unfortunately, are reaping the threats and the anger from people's reactions to that technique. They were following that technique which is allowed, so let's talk more about the system, I guess. I was hoping, and do hope, that instead of threatening police officers who weren't really violating the laws.

Q. I think the biggest amount of feedback we got was about how he was interrogated for hours without any support with him in the room, such as a lawyer or parent because he wasn't of legal age. How could his interview stand up in court?

A. Here's where it really gets fact-specific, Al. Apparently, the mother chose not to be there in the first interview. Remember, there are about three or four interviews, and *Making a Murderer* only showed one of them. As far as his lawyer not being there, that is malpractice per se, you know, ridiculous. But I don't think that was the confession used, either.

So, some of the premises that people are upset about are not true. I'm not trying to say that even what they used in the trial should be the way that the law allows it. You can make an argument that any juvenile should always be required to have a parent there. Even if the parent says no, the law says the juvenile doesn't have to be there; there would be a lot of shootings and armed robberies that would go unsolved or even murders. That would be the result if there was an absolute prohibition against that. So, it needs to be balanced and weighed out.

His case, whether it did cross the line, is open to interpretation. I guess the court will look at it, though. Not just what the viewers looked at in *Making a Murderer*. The court will look at which particular interview was introduced into evidence. Not the really shaky, dicey ones where he was not served with effective assistance of counsel. In fact, he was sabotaged. Probably well intended by his counsel and the counsel's private investigators.

But there's an interview before that the

court will have to try and figure out if it was coercive or not. If it was coercive, it gets suppressed, and he gets a new trial. And I would think that there's nothing there with which to use as evidence against Brendan Dassey. So, it might be his time in prison is done. It is what the case law is; whatever the case law and court find is rules of evidence and presented for it, not a documentary, and that's the anger that's expressed.

Q. I will say that the documentary made the officers who were doing the interrogation look bad straight across the board. What I mean by that is they didn't show us anything from their perspective. When you make people look evil throughout the whole series, then that's what people think they are.

A. You know it does look bad, a police officer interrogating. And sometimes it is bad. There are some officers that do it in a fairer way. I'm not going to weigh in on what Fassbender did. But I can say that what they showed was the worst of what those two cops did. I had some cops whose interviewing techniques I can't stand and I don't use, and I wish they weren't police officers. I don't think Wiegert and Fassbender are in that club. I don't work with them; they are in different jurisdictions. But I've seen worse. But recognizing this, please listeners, you did not see the whole thing; you saw the worst parts of the interview.

With Dassey, I don't disagree necessarily with a lot of the viewers of *Making a Murderer*. Certainly, the troubling aspect of it and that they're troubled by. We'll just see what the justice system does if we get to the point that we don't trust at all the justice system courts and the appellant process and rules of evidence and constitutional principals that have been around since, whatever, sixteen hundred in England. It's not perfect, but if we assume it's all corrupt and *Making a Murderer* and documentaries like this are all correct, you can't look further. Or you got to accept that version and not trust the courts, whatever, at every level, we're in trouble.

Q. My only other question about the Dassey interview was when the officer asked him, "Who shot Teresa Halbach?" Now, most of the feedback I received about that was the officer was giving Dassey the information that Halbach was indeed shot. Is that okay to be used in the trial?

A. My understanding was that Brendan had said something about the gun and shooting Miss Halbach—Avery shooting Miss Halbach—before that interview. In an interview that I think was used in the trial and was not shown on *Making a Murderer*. Now, lets fact check that. I'll fact-check when we're done, and I'm sure your listeners will fact-check that. I'm almost certain, at least, that's what a person I know, a law enforcement officer, reminded me of the other day, and if that person's wrong, I will be talking to that person. But, I think he had stated in a prior interview that's not shown in *Making a Murderer* that I think was also said in court that Dassey had told the police that Steven Avery had shot Teresa Halbach. I don't know if he said, "in the head," but I believe there was mention of a gun and shooting.

Q. In the prosecution of the first Steven Avery case, what were the things that bothered you most about that trial?

A. Lots. Number one, the prosecutor lied to his staff. His staff came up and said, "Hey, I think it's Gregory Allan. Looks like him, sounds like him." The prosecutor at the time in 1985 said, "Well, I checked, the Sheriff checked, and Gregory Allan, the real assailant, was on probation. He's on probation still, and his agent told me he's got an airtight alibi, so it can't be Allan."

Well, the Attorney General found that actually, Allan wasn't even on probation. There are a number of other things, including a complaint I found in the Avery file showing that the same prosecutor, whom I name in the book, Dennis Vogel, had prosecuted the real assailant, Gregory Allan, back in 1985 for trying to attack a woman. Lunging at her, dropping his shorts on the same section of beach that Penny Berntsen was attacked two years later by Mr. Allan.

There was other evidence. I believe a leather jacket, and I believe some police witnesses perjured themselves about seeing Avery wearing a leather jacket on various occasions when they had contact with him a few prior years. Penny had described a particular leather jacket on the assailant. The Sheriff knew the DA knew, very likely within a couple of days, that Avery didn't do it.

There's other evidence to that, too, that gets pretty densely packed in here that we don't have time for it here. They knew Gregory Allan did it, which is just as bad or worse, I don't know which. They're both bad. They kept going against Mr. Avery and put him away for eighteen years for a crime he didn't do. And let Mr. Allan go free, and Allan brutally raped a woman in Green Bay eight years after escaping responsibility for attacking and almost killing Penny Berntsen.

Those guys remain unaccounted for this, the two, the Sheriff and the DA. They dodged a bullet—a wrongful conviction lawsuit—when they were personally sued. They got a pass from the Wisconsin Attorney General when she found no criminal violations, and they're still not getting any heat. It's the current officers who weren't even there at the time and who were involved in this case because of an investigation that happened on their watch. But they are paying, essentially, for the sins of their predecessors, and their predecessors are skating free. It's troubling in a lot of ways.

Q. In the *Making a Murderer* series, some of the cops there are accused of planting the evidence against Steven Avery, and a lot of people are convinced of that. They are the same officers who were deposed in the first case for the lawsuit, and they happen to find the evidence against Avery. Do you know if any of them are still working on the force today?

A. One of them is retired and did retire probably five years ago, Jim Lenk, and the other, Andy Colborn, is still a detective for the Sheriff's department. But neither of them was there in 1985 when Mr. Avery was wrongly convicted for the first time. Second of all, they were not sued, they were not parties in the wrongful conviction lawsuit, and they were witnesses.

They received a call, and that's why they were being deposed. I think Colborn was just a corrections officer at the time, and Lenk was probably a deputy at the time in 1995 – ten years after the time when Mr. Avery was wrongly convicted. Yet this call from Green Bay PD saying, and this is at night, you know, second or third shift, saying, "Hey, there's an inmate we have who's saying he did this crime, and you got the wrong guy in prison for it," and they kind of referenced the crime on the beach.

So, my guess is that they didn't even know Colborn, and Lenk didn't even know that it was the Berntsen case or the Avery case because I don't think they even used the name. But they did what they should; frankly, they passed it up the line to the hierarchy, and the hierarchy said, "No, tell them that we don't want to hear it. We got our guy, and we don't know what they're talking about." So, Colborn and Lenk had no reason to believe that Avery, this guy who was in prison before they were even there, was wrongly convicted. They were doing what the higher-up, probably the Sheriff himself, who is escaping responsibility for this, told them to do.

But the timing is horrible. I think it was three or four weeks after their deposition that Teresa disappeared and was murdered, and they shouldn't have been in the trailer. Let's face it. They did not belong in the trailer. They presented worse in the documentary than it was. There was a county cop with them the whole time. The documentary only shows the final question by the defense, where the county cop admits that "It's possible that they could have been alone, or when I looked away, they could have planted the key."

Of course, the documentary shows an empty bookcase with the key on the floor. The fact is, the bookcase was not empty when they pulled it away. They pulled away a full, jammed with magazines and books. They were looking through that, those things for evidence, which I'm not able to say. Well, pornography is essentially what they thought would be relevant, depending on what they found, to the trial. This was weeks after the murder.

It was while jamming the stuff back, and I believe this was in the testimony, in jamming the stuff back, the fake backing of this thing, or cheap backing, pulled away, and the key dropped out. So, what does *Making a Murderer* show? They show an empty bookcase with the key on the ground as if nobody could have missed it earlier. Totally manipulates the viewer.

Q. What were those officers doing at Avery's trailer anyways? I thought you guys working in your county had been called off. This is another feedback issue: why did they go there to investigate when another county's police department is taking care of it?

A. Right, they shouldn't have been. The District Attorney and myself, we were there. My new boss because I helped a lot as he was brand new. We were called to the scene when it was still a missing person when her car was found, and I was there for several hours. Until the remains of Teresa, the dog hit on those, then it became a homicide. An official homicide case.

Everyone suspected that we would find Teresa's remains there, but there was no guarantee of that. But at that point, when we know it's a homicide, and let's face it Avery, and the police might have denied it but, he was the main suspect. He called her out there, so let's call apples, apples, and oranges, oranges.

But he wasn't the only suspect. By the way, they got the DNA from all of the other Averys too. But he was the main suspect, and as soon as Teresa's remains were found, the DA backed off and left. I left, and I don't know if he left immediately. The police are onto themselves. The Sheriff's department thought that with the size of the Calumet county force, which is probably only about a fourth of Manitowoc

County, it would probably be kind of tough for them to search that whole property.

So, the Sheriff, or whoever, decided to compromise and can't. You either have a conflict, or you don't. You're either pregnant, or you're not. But, they decided they would not have any Manitowoc County officers search. And they should have never had any Manitowoc officers involved in the search of the resident's actual residence. Outbuildings maybe, or the cars, thousands of cars, that's where they should have focused them. But they didn't, and here we are.

Q. Another major point that people seem to be talking about is that when they tried the two suspects, Avery and Dassey, separately, they also prosecuted them with different scenarios. In the Dassey trial, they went with what he confessed to, that they tied Halbach to Avery's bed in his bedroom, raped her, then stabbed her in her stomach, but yet there was no blood found in Avery's room. Meanwhile, for the Avery trial, they didn't use any of that or even Dassey at all.

A. Right, I understand that. I've read that in various places too. For the person who doesn't do criminal law or litigation, I get why they think that. The fact is, the prosecution could not mention anything about Dassey or about Dassey's statement as to how the murder happened. That would be a mistrial because Brendan Dassey never cut a deal with the state. Therefore, he had a fifth amendment right not to incriminate himself, and the state could not use him or his testimony in the Avery case.

The way it works puts us in a weird position sometimes as prosecutors and defense lawyers too. You have to only argue only the evidence admitted into court, i.e. that's allowed into court. So, the state, in the Avery case, could not say anything about how Teresa died. They couldn't know anything about the knifing, the shooting in the bedroom, the torture, etc. All they could talk about was the physical evidence found in the circumstance of the Avery case. So, Steven Avery called out to get Teresa there, asking specifically that she be the one to come to his residence or junkyard to take the pictures.

So, it was a circumstantial case and a physical evidence case in the trial of Avery. Brendan Dassey's case was the exact opposite. If I recall correctly, there was no physical evidence tying Dassey to the murder. It was all his own statements.

You know, there have been false confession cases where the person confessed, but counter-intuitively they confessed to something they didn't do. Did that happen in Brendan Dassey's case? Some people think it did. I don't know. I don't believe it did. I looked at all four hours of videotaped confession, and I don't believe it did.

If I only watched *Making a Murderer*, I think I'd walk away like a lot of the viewers, but the majority of viewers did. Again, that's for a court to decide. Brendan Dassey has a right, an absolute right, and this time to effective counsel. Arguing that the confession was coerced out of him, and secondarily, in addition to being coerced, may be false. Although even if it was a true confession, if it were coerced under the law against his constitutional rights, he deserves a new trial. Maybe even be released, as there is no other evidence as far as I know. But I think it's important that he gets his day in court and that Mr. Avery get his day in court too.

Q. When we talk about blood evidence with the Avery case and the blood sample and issues surrounding that, such as the sample being left and not being sealed correctly, is that kind of stuff common, or is that something that we should be suspicious about?

A. My understanding is that it is very common. When you draw blood in a forensic sense, in a criminal case, and you are preserving the blood in a test tube to send it to a hygiene lab or a crime lab to test it, what you do is draw the blood from the person through a tube into a test tube, through a plastic tube that is, into the main test tube, the blood vial itself, you do it through a needle that goes through the stopper or the cap of it.

Again, *Making a Murderer* makes it seem like it's a shocking discovery. They don't explain the rest, which the defense knew at the time. The seal, I don't know enough about it. I suspect that the seal, you know, that blood, had been tested and opened. That blood had been tested a lot and opened a lot because of the appeals in Avery's case. So, I think, once again, there's been a misrepresentation about what the blood vial in that condition means.

Q. Was there anything about the second case shown in the *Making a Murderer* series that was suspicious to you, or do you think it was all reasonable?

A. The key bothered me. It just looks too strange. But in looking through it further, it had been eight years since any of us had followed this case. I wasn't the prosecutor; I hope people remember that. I am from the area, and I didn't have time to watch the entire trial. I have a caseload to deal with, like domestic abuse and drunk driving. It's Wisconsin, after all, so there's lots of drunk driving, robberies, etc. But I knew enough about it at the time.

I especially knew enough about Brendan Dassey's confession, and perhaps that's why I was so certain in my first book, *The Innocent Killer,* of Avery's guilt. Nobody really questioned it. I still don't question it because now I know a lot more, and I looked into it a lot more. But on the first watch, yeah. If you watch just what they had before you, you start to wonder how that key, how did those guys end up there, and boy, that looks fishy. You got to look further. That's all I'm saying. That's up to your listeners.

From my Facebook page and other things that are going on with me, including threats and ugly things, I suspect, well, I know that a certain amount of your listeners who feel strongest about this won't listen to anything I say. And you know that's their right. It's too bad, and I don't think it's the way to approach trying to find the truth. But if people are really interested in the truth, they'll keep the personal stuff out. Maybe I come off as all-knowing or something, and if I do, I'm sorry. But I'm speaking as a flawed human being like everybody else.

Q. I think there have been many things lately that have made people very emotional, and this is just one of those things that are a trigger.

A. I think you're right, Al. But most people don't approach it that way. There's a sizeable, very vocal group that does, and some of it has gotten out of hand. There were bomb threats at the jail the other day that was going to get the Sheriff's office and the court house which is only about fifty feet away. Colborn gets a call on Christmas Day, just trying to celebrate with his family, that was threatening his wife. A couple of cops threatened on the job, you know, people yelling Avery. Punched at and worse, I'm not even scratching the surface of this.

I do get the passion and emotion. Most of it is fueled by a really interesting show. A great draw-you-in kind of documentary. Their show, personally, I think, needs to be a little more accurate. Well done, to be sure, and probably well intended for the most part. The criminal justice system is pretty screwed up in a lot of ways, so raising these issues, including the issue that it's hard for people who are less blessed in life. Economically, you know, social, economic classes to get a fair shake in the criminal justice system.

My only point is they didn't have the whole thing. They had a one-sided portrayal. You don't put on Steven Avery's prior cat-burning incident, and this is when he was twenty-two, not younger, as they kind of imply. You don't suggest that that was just an accident horsing around with friends where he was just throwing up the cat, and it ended up in the fire. You don't do that when in fact, he was twenty-two, and he doused the cat with gasoline and intentionally threw it in the fire. The cat died, and he pled to animal cruelty.

Or the incident with the ramming the woman in the car with his pick-up truck and holding her at gunpoint after she lost control of the car. You don't portray that as he's just getting back at her because she was spreading rumors about him and his family. She probably was. But in fact, he had been watching her for months with a pair of binoculars. Essentially stalking her. Watching her get into her car from up the street in the morning early, driving by occasionally. He would, well, often, he would sexually gratify himself as she drove by. One time, well more than once, he even ran into the highway in front of her car nude. He only let her go after he held a rifle to her head when she pointed out that she had an infant in the back seat of the car, so Steven let her go. He pled to that offense, by the way, not a sex offense because he did let her go and not assault her.

Q. Now, the makers of the film say that they offered the prosecution to take part in the series, but they declined. Why did they do that?

A. Well, I took part in it, but I understand what you're saying and that you mean Kratz. I was in the first episode mostly because I think I wrote the book about Mr. Avery's first case when the police wrongly convicted him in a bad way. But *Making a Murderer* said that because they did probably ask the prosecution, and Kratz probably said no. They may have thought there might be some ethical issues in doing that while trying the case. Kratz didn't seem to be real shy about talking to the press, though. In my book, I refer to him as "Ken, I-never-saw-a-camera-I-didn't-like Kratz."

I think one of the police officers, Colborn, did actually want to talk to them, or at least did want to talk to the press, but the crown lawyer, I believe, suggested that he didn't. You know there's a cautiousness in the government, too, that has not served them well. But yeah, I suppose, I don't know that just saying that we asked them to and they just wouldn't talk means that you were objective when you recorded it.

Q. What do you think is next for Steven Avery with his new lawyer?

A. She certainly is an accomplished, talented, skilled attorney, and she has not been shy at all about what she thinks she can do and has done in the past. So, everybody's got their different styles, I guess. I imagine she'll be filing a motion for a new trial. I don't know when. I imagine there'll be plenty of ammunition that she'll have to throw out there, and I'll guess we'll all wait and see what it is. I don't believe that there is anything because I believe the evidence clearly matches the beyond reasonable doubt that he did it. I'd be shocked if she's got something to suggest he didn't.

But then there's the question of did he get a fair trial which is somewhat separate in a way, and I think, legally, that's an easy call in Steven Avery's case. I think he absolutely got a fair trial. I know your listeners who only watched *Making a Murderer* don't believe that.

Listen to the full interview with Michael Griesbach on my website:

https://www.alanrwarren.com/
hom-podcast-episodes/
episode/74fabc50/michael-
griesbach-steven-avery

Part Three

THE DEFENSE

Chapter 7
Interview with Shawn Rech

I n the Fall of 2019, filmmaker Shawn Rech started making the press tour talking about the release of his new documentary called *Convicting a Murderer*. The documentary is centered around the Steven Avery and Brendan

Dassey convictions for the murder of Teresa Halbach, which had been the topic in the popular Netflix documentary *Making a Murderer*.

During his media blitz, Rech claimed to have spent eighteen months making a ten-part series that fact-checked the information shown in the *Making a Murderer* series. Rech also says that in his series, you will see the law enforcement point of view as well, as it was not seen in the original series. There is also supposed to be some new information uncovered during the making of this series.

Shawn Rech is a documentary filmmaker, director, and producer. Rech has focused his filmmaking career on covering wrongful convictions and discussing the sentencing process. His best-known film, *A Murder in the Park*, made for Showtime and Netflix, was listed by *Time Magazine* in their top fifteen most fascinating true crime stories ever to be told.

I sat down with Shawn Rech on October 19, 2019, to learn more about this new series and to go deeper into the project than the short news briefs floating around the internet.

Q. You've been making your own film or series called *Convicting a Murderer*. What is the purpose behind it?

A. The long and short of it is I watched *Making a Murderer* season one. It was really interesting. I was really entertained. It was good for filmmakers like me who do true crime, and it broke new ground, and I was excited by it.

Then, I started doing some studying, and I learned that in many ways, I, the viewer, was misled, and they left a lot of information on the table. They also steered people the wrong way in some instances. They don't consider themselves journalists, but this was advocacy journalism without the transparency and with some really unethical strands in which they went when they told this story.

So, I fully waited for someone to correct the record. After a couple of years, it didn't appear that anyone was going to do it. So, I said well, we're up for the challenge. That's why we set out to kind of make a more complete version.

Q. It's frustrating for me too. I watched it as well, and I walked away thinking that they were framed and he probably didn't do it. But when I interviewed people like Ken Kratz, I started to realize that not only is there more evidence that was not shown, but there are things that have been changed in the series to make it look one way while it was really something else. So, this is no longer a documentary or journalism.

A. No, it's kind of like the old show back in the eighties that no one watched, remember, called *Not Necessarily the News*.

Q. I remember that!

A. Yes, just take those soundbites and have Ronald Reagan saying his pants were on fire. Some of the editing is that bad, and they won an Emmy for editing. Creative editing.

Q. For me, it's too Alex Jonesy, and as soon as you do that, you've created false evidence. You've created a narrative that's not true. So, how can we trust anything in the whole series?

A. The weird thing is that they're not asking you to trust them because once they were confronted, I mean with just the beginning when people found out, they said, "Hey, we're not journalists." We created entertainment, and everybody is wildly entertained. Forty million people watched this thing. It turned Netflix around a little bit, was kind of stagnant, and they began to grow again. It had a profound effect.

Well, guess what? It also had a profound effect on the lives of these guys you painted as crooked cops and crooked prosecutors who set out to bury these guys. They did a lot of things that affected people. They left me with the impression that the Averys were poor, but that's not true. They left me with the impression that Manitowoc was a bleak, kind of like a sad town. Kind of like an Ozark meth paradise kind of place. And that's not true at all. It's a beautiful town.

There's just item after item. There's so much that we literally have meetings now deciding what to include and what not to include because we don't want to overwhelm people.

Q. We have been interviewing a lot of the players who were involved in this case, such as Ken Kratz. After the show aired, we got a ton of hate emails and messages just for doing the interview. How do you think you can overcome that rage? Are they even going to watch your series, and if they do, will they really listen to what you have to say in it?

A. Yeah, with Ken, we've got an internal saying, even when he wins, he loses. We thought that the pacing of *Making a Murderer* was really slow, you know, by watching grandpa eat lettuce for thirty seconds. Maybe, it was a little too arthouse? We were going to go at a faster pace. So, one of the things that we wanted to do was to get these people who lust to salivate and say, man, if I could just get at that guy. We are connecting him (Kratz) with that guy and putting them in a room and letting them go at it and have this kind of debate and discussion.

We had a guy come in, and we got a courtroom, and the guy made some points, and Kratz made some points. But Kratz, even when he was right, just sometimes does it in a way that leaves people sort of disliking him. Like, of course, I'm right, you jerk. It's because he's so frustrated. He's just passed the limit of being nice because his son's life has been threatened a couple of hundred times, and his wife's been insulted a thousand times. I got thirty-seven audio CDs of threats and death threats made to people in this case. We are going to weave them into the series every now and then just for flavor.

Another fascinating thing to me is that we're going to tell everybody that the blood vial was BS. And you know, Steven really did kill his cat. He didn't just steal a cheese sandwich, but he tore up this business and some of these other things. Part of the wrongful conviction time was for a legitimate kidnapping, where he pointed a gun at a child.

We're going to tell them all this stuff. But the funny thing is the hardcore truthers, like those who are on Reddit or Twitter, already know this. They've moved way beyond anything they saw in *Making a Murderer*. I said this in the press in another interview a couple of weeks ago. I've checked Twitter, and they say, of course, "We've moved on. That's old news." This is their life. They've really got the pulse of this case, and they've got new theories all the time. It's funny *Making a Murderer* started all of this, but they know that most of what they saw is horse crap.

Q. It's harder to 'unconvince' people of something than it is to convince them. I think a lot of people are trapped in that because that's the first place they went and the first thing they heard.

A. We thought something that would be useful was to interview some of these people who were unconvinced themselves. Converts. But to some of these folks, this would be like joining the Communist Party in the sixties. So, we have them explain their thought process about what raised the red flags. That doesn't mean that we necessarily agree with them. That doesn't mean that we think that Steven Avery should stay in prison. I sure don't think that Brendan Dassey should stay in prison.

Q. Do you think that Brendan Dassey should be out of prison because you believe he had nothing to do with the crime or because you think he was incapable of defending himself because he was slow or improper counsel during the trial?

A. My issue is that he was mentally incapable of initiating anything like this, in my opinion. If he was involved, he was a follower. He was taking orders, and he was subordinate to his uncle if, in fact, it happened that way. He's done enough time. He's not going to get out and go stalk and kill someone. He's going to go fishing, play video games, and go to WrestleMania. I don't think society has anything to worry about with the release of Brendan Dassey.

I'll tell you one chilling thing. When we interviewed Len Kachinsky, who, interestingly enough, I didn't realize, in *Making a Murderer*, he's a judge. Well, he's an inmate now, but he was put in jail the other day for some allegations. I interviewed him and asked him if he felt bad for Brendan or do he wish he was out now. He looked at the camera and said, "Not particularly." There's somebody with no empathy. He made a terrible mistake leaving him with that want-to-be-a-cop investigator.

Q. But I think that's what ruined his reputation. That part of the series was all true, correct?

A. Yes, sure it is. Brendan came up with things before that, but you could say that he was led because that's the Reid method, where they suggest somewhat during the interview. But he came up with things without being led, also. So people need to take that into consideration. But whatever happened, this is enough time for him.

Q. Sergeant Colborn was another person that was vilified in the series. What can you tell us about him?

A. What people don't realize, yes, he was a witness in the wrongful conviction case because he took a phone call when he was a corrections officer before he was a full-fledged cop. He took a call where somebody said we think you've got the wrong guy and he forwarded the call to the detective bureau. When he heard about Avery being found innocent, he volunteered that information that he took this call.

So, in a sense, he was a witness for Avery. On his own, his coming forward would help Avery's case. Everyone acts like he was on the hook and going to lose millions in this lawsuit, and of course, he planted the key. Well, no, he believes Steven Avery is innocent of the Beerntsen rape, and he was fascinated that the DNA could exonerate him. He thought there was a whole new era coming that was going to make crime easier to fight because of DNA. He just didn't have a vested interest in burying Steven Avery. The way they portrayed him as being involved in the old case was a real mischaracterization.

Q. What other egregious misrepresentations can you cite in the documentary for people who may not be familiar with the truth of the case?

A. What we are going to show is actual footage of some depositions and some courtroom scenes, and then we are going to show the *Making a Murderer* edit. I believe it's going to make viewers' blood boil because it's not an accident. It's not for the sake of entertainment. It is a deliberately misleading direction that they took with people. I was angry when I saw some of the stuff, and I think a lot of viewers will be too.

Q. When you say it's deliberately misleading, what was the reason for that? Was it because they wanted to hurt cops, or what was their motive?

A. No. I think the cops were the damage on the periphery. Collateral damage. They wanted to get their guy off. We have prison recordings of them talking to him. They came and left every day with the family. They were embedded with the family. They picked sides. It's okay. I picked sides too. But you have to be transparent about it, and you have to be fair. They were neither. They were not transparent as far as their advocacy, and they weren't fair, and I'm going to go as far as say they weren't honest.

Q. It's really too bad because now when people go to watch a documentary in the future, they're going to become untrustworthy.

A. Right! And it was one of the biggest documentaries ever on crime. There was *The Jinx* and *Making a Murderer*. *The Jinx* was honest. *Making a Murderer* was not. We've got to correct the record. We've got to make some ground rules because I see us as the new long-form deep-dive journalism.

Young people want visual news. They want to hear it, or they want to see it. They want authenticity. And newspapers and magazines, besides the fact that they're dying, aren't spending the money on real journalism anyway and are letting all of their good people go because they cost money. When you go to the network, all they're doing is choir preaching. It's all just Trump all day, loving him or hating him. So, there's a gap, and we have the opportunity to become journalists. To fill in that gap.

When one of the biggest, most important documentaries pulls the crap that they pulled, we have to correct the record. It's probably going to bore some people who made us arbitrators of what's honest. We're just saying that it should be held to journalistic standards or at least disclose certain things and not lie. That's why the record has to be corrected. We really feel the need to do this.

Q. Who is going to regulate this? This wasn't the first documentary to lie. The *Soaked in Bleach* movie about Kurt Cobain's death did the same thing. They edited the answers of their guests to say what they wanted people to believe. And I interviewed several of the people who were in their movie, and they all said the same thing, that they never said what is portrayed in that movie. So, *Making a*

Murderer wasn't the first one. They are just the most prominent one. How can we reign that in? Because there's a lot of money to be made by promoting a conspiracy.

A. Yeah, well, you're right. Oliver Stone, even with scripted features, you can do it. I think it's going to be up to the audience. I think that they want authenticity. I think that there are still people out there who can vouch for the credibility of what you are doing or saying.

When *Making a Murderer* came out, the *New Yorker,* two weeks later, had a long-form article saying, "Hold on, before you make fools of yourself, you need to know this about *Making a Murderer.*" But not that many people around the world read the *New Yorker*. I read the piece, and that's what started me on my path.

I went, wait a minute, there was never anything to the blood. That was almost a whole episode. The thing ended, and I was wondering why the blood wasn't in court. It was because it was a non-issue, and they knew it was a non-issue.

Q. Well, all of this begs the question that I just have to ask you. The changes in editing people's statements and leaving out important information, selective omissions, and all of that, doesn't that indicate that the people who made the documentary are aware of the problem that you are talking about? They know what they're doing, right?

A. In my opinion, yes. Now, Andy Colborn, whose courtroom testimony was changed in *Making a Murderer*, filed suit. I don't know if the suit is going to survive. There are a lot of procedural reasons that it may or may not. But if he gets his day in court, they are going to show an edit where they ask him a very important question, and the *Making a Murderer* viewer sees him say yes. But he never said yes. He never answered the question. They took the yes answer from a different question. That's not a mistake. That's not entertainment. That's just egregious.

Q. Joseph Evans Jr., I just roll my eyes because I think it's way too obvious. First of all, he claims that he got a confession from Steven Avery for murdering Teresa Halbach when they were in prison together. Next thing, there's a large reward for information on the case by Kathleen

Zellner, Avery's lawyer now, and now Evans claims that he murdered Halbach.

A. Let me tell you, I did press for two and a half weeks on this. Let me tell you something that I didn't tell anybody. He sent that letter, and the letter had all of this supplemental information. We were trying to fact-check a lot of it. Part of it was that Steve had a bag that had some stuff in it that he had buried. It was something that we were investigating. Then the detectives up north in Manitowoc County saw a bag when they first questioned him and never checked it. The next time they pulled over his vehicle, the bag was gone. We figured that we were going to have to look for that bag. We had to think about some logical places where he might have buried it. We had professional metal detectors and spent thousands of dollars looking for them. We did all of this crap just based on this clown's letter.

There were some other things in the letter that I thought told us that the letter wasn't legit. In the letter, Evans claimed that Steven Avery told him that he couldn't talk about the case anymore because Netflix was making a documentary. I was going to say to him, look, Netflix wasn't making a documentary. They acquired this years later. A couple of young filmmakers were making a documentary. So, why did you say that? That's an example of something being informed by hindsight which tells me this whole letter may be informed by hindsight.

So, I called Evans, and he said let me tell you what happened. He went to Avery's Salvage Yard to buy a window and hit Teresa with his car. He panicked because he was on so many drugs. He decided to frame the homeowner, whom he didn't know, and he goes through every little point trying to show that he framed Steven Avery.

Of course, now we know that his motive was that he was trying to get his girlfriend that $100,000 reward. He killed his wife, so you have to take it seriously because he's a killer. And he was free when Teresa was killed. And he was there in the area. It's worth a little bit of follow-up, but I was upset because we wasted a lot of money.

Q. What is it that you want the viewers of your documentary to walk away with?

A. I want them to walk away with a full understanding of what happened. I want them to walk away with a law enforcement perspective because those guys didn't cooperate with *Making a Murderer*.

Q. What it comes down to also is that if Steven Avery is actually innocent and he was framed, they should be able to make that case with the truth, right?

A. Absolutely. This is what I told the law enforcement guys who agreed to be interviewed. I said if we find some evidence that you guys did wrong, we will march the guy out with his attorneys. We will run to them with the evidence. We're not going to withhold something that could be that relevant.

Shawn Rech's movie for Transition Studios was ultimately called *Convicting* is in post-production Convicting - Transition Studios

Listen to the full interview with Shawn Rech on my website:

https://www.alanrwarren.com/
hom-podcast-episodes/
episode/1a9b90a3/convicting-
a-murderer-shawn-rech

Chapter 8
Interview with Laura Nirider

Laura Nirider is an attorney and an associate law professor at Northwestern University. From 2009 to 2019, Nirider was the co-director of the Center on Wrongful Convictions of Youth. During those ten years, she became an expert on how children get coerced into giving false confessions for crimes they didn't commit.

Nirider believes that the intention of interrogation aims to get information from people who are often hostile towards law enforcement. Police also have to interview people who can be unstable or very vulnerable. Currently, there are no specific standards for interrogating them, so their reactions to the methods are, at best unreliable.

Nirider first gained the public's attention when she was co-counsel to Damien Echols, a member of what became known as the "West Memphis Three," who had initially been sentenced to death for murder. Eventually, with Nirider's aid, Echols was released in 2011.

On the last episode of *Making a Murderer*, Nirider was featured as she was brought in to try to remove the Brendan Dassey confession as evidence since it is believed he was not only coerced by interrogators but also had no counsel or parent in the room during his interviews.

In the second season of Netflix's *Making a Murderer*, Nirider's defense of Dassey is prominently covered. I figured this would be the perfect time to see what Nirider thought about the Dassey case and the current justice system.

This interview took place on October 19, 2020.

Q. Let's talk about how you got involved with the Innocence Project?

A. It's a question that has everything to do with my representation of Brendan Dassey. For me, it goes back thirteen years, when I was a law student here at Northwestern University in Chicago. I was getting near the end of law school, and I had my full life figured out. I was going to be a business lawyer. That was my plan. I had a job lined up after graduation. On my last day of law school, on a whim, I decided to sign up for a class on wrongful convictions.

I knew nothing about criminal law. I knew nothing about the justice system. And I certainly knew nothing about wrongful convictions. This just happened to be about four months after Dassey had been convicted in Wisconsin for raping and murdering Teresa Halbach. My professor, Steve, had disagreed with handling Brendan Dassey's appeal because he's an expert on false confessions.

A couple of weeks into the Fall semester, Steve called me into his office, and he said I'd just gotten involved in the case of a young man from Wisconsin, sixteen years old and intellectually disabled, who confessed to a murder that I don't think he committed. Then he handed me the interrogation videos of Brendan Dassey. The same videos that years later would end up on *Making a Murderer*. He told me to go home and watch them.

So, I go and sit down on my couch, take out my laptop, and I put in these DVDs, and I watch them all from start to finish. My heart broke because I saw two adults, police officers, manipulating a sixteen-year-old special education student into confessing to a murder that he couldn't even describe. I knew I couldn't walk away. That did it for me.

I graduated, and I came back to Northwestern. Within a few months, I started building, alongside Steve, the Center for Wrongful Convictions, where I started representing Brendan and a lot of other people just like him.

Q. There are a lot of false confessions that happen for different reasons. But quite often, when we cover a false confession, a lot of the listeners' responses will be, "I would never confess to something that I never did." They don't believe the person claiming this. How do you overcome such an argument?

A. That's exactly the right question to ask, why would anyone confess to a crime they didn't commit? Especially something as brutal as rape or murder. Of course, all of us think I wouldn't do that, so what's the matter with this person who did? This is part of what fascinated me, so I started learning about false confessions and police interrogations.

It turns out that the answer to this question of why anyone would falsely confess has a lot to do with the psychology of the interrogation room. It has a lot to do with the psychological tactics that police officers are trained to use inside the interrogation room.

Basically speaking, the interrogation has two phases. The first phase is about reducing the suspect down to hopelessness. You're caught. You're trapped. You're cornered. And you have no way out. Your life is over, and you're going down for this.

The second half is about offering a confession as a life raft, right? You're caught, but if you confess, people will understand that you are a good person and that you have remorse. They'll want to help you. They'll see that you are cooperating and so on. That is what you'll see in a lot of these interrogations that result in a false confession, and I have watched hundreds of these videos and represented dozens of these people.

You see this basic structure of interrogation get cranked up, get amped up in ways that would affect any of us. For example, police officers lie about the evidence against the suspect, which most people don't know is perfectly legal in the United States but not in many other countries. But it's totally legal here. So, you'll see officers say, "You're trying to tell us you're innocent, but we found your DNA at the scene," or, "We found your fingerprints on the gun."

Then you can see the suspects start to think to themselves, "My God, how is this possible? I've never been to the crime scene. But this cop says he's got my DNA. He really thinks I did this. What am I going to do?" You see those sorts of lies in the interrogation room, and once the suspect feels cornered or trapped—hopeless —you'll see officers say, "Look, if you don't confess, you'll get the death penalty. Or you'll get life in prison. But if you do confess, we'll be able to help you."

You can see how these tactics combined over the course of many hours, sometimes overnight, to make a suspect think that they have no way out of this horrific situation but to confess. These are really powerful tactics. They are very good at getting true confessions from guilty people. They are so powerful that they can also get false confessions.

Q. So, what's the answer to that, then? How can we fix this?

A. Yeah, how can we fix this, or how can we do better? That's exactly the right question to ask. One of the things that I do is I work really closely with police and prosecutors, and it's not about attacking them. It's about learning from these cases. At the end of the day, nobody wants an innocent person behind bars while the guilty person is out on the streets. Nobody wants that.

So, that's a big part of what I do. I gather these interrogation videos, I study these cases, and I work closely with law enforcement to figure out better ways of doing things. It turns out that when you look at these cases and study them, you don't need to lie about evidence in the interrogation room to get a confession. You don't need to use death threats. There are way better techniques out there that are more based on rapport-building. They are more based on conversational techniques that are very good at solving crimes and are being used in other countries all the time.

You know, one of the fascinating things about the techniques that I describe is the way interrogation works right now in all fifty states. These are commonly used interrogation techniques. One of the fascinating things is that these techniques were developed seventy years ago, in the forties and fifties. At the time, they were thought of as revolutionary because they replaced physical abuse in the interrogation room. It was the kindler, gentler way of getting to the truth.

What's interesting now is that we've had another leap in our thinking now that DNA has been invented. It turns out we have been proving confessions false using DNA at a rate that's much higher than anybody ever thought and under circumstances that are different than anybody thought before. So, it's time for us to learn from what these cases can tell us, from what the DNA revolution can tell us, and it's time to work together to move this forward.

Q. When I look at the Brendan Dassey case and the whole *Making a Murderer* series, it all seems to come down to a cult of personality in everyone who was involved in the Avery case. For example, look at Ken Kratz, where the majority of people who have watched the series absolutely hate him. I have had him on the show two or three times, and to this day, he still swears by Dassey being involved in Teresa Halbach's murder. Do you think he actually believes this, or is it too difficult for him to admit that he's wrong, as it hurts his pride?

A. I can't speak to what's in someone else's head, but what I can say is that when you have worked on as many false confession cases as I have, and that my colleagues and I have, these are cases where confessions have been proven false by DNA where we know they were false, you see the exact same thing play out in those cases. Old-school law enforcement, who may not necessarily mean any harm whatsoever and may really want to get the real perpetrator or keep them behind bars.

Old-school law enforcement has a really hard time adjusting to this new reality where false confessions really happen. They happen under circumstances that are different than you think. It doesn't take special abuse, especially for someone like Brendan Dassey. It doesn't take heavy-handed techniques. Brendan was sixteen and in special ed. He's in tenth grade, and one of his special ed. accommodations in school, in his classroom, was that he needed an adult to sit with him so that he could understand the words the teachers were saying to him. His disabilities were really verbal. He had a really hard time understanding the spoken word. So, he needed this adult with him in the classroom to help him cope with that.

When you put a kid like that in an interrogation room and bombard him with five or six questions per minute for hours and hours and hours with no adult, no lawyer, no parent, no nothing by his side, these are exactly the kind of circumstances that you see in hundreds of cases across the country that can lead to false confessions.

One of the key moments, the hardest but one of the most important, that was shown in *Making a Murderer* from Brendan's interrogation is when he was trying to guess how Teresa Halbach was killed, and he can't get it right. He guesses all these different ways of killing somebody. The officers keep telling him he's getting it wrong. Finally, Brendan has no idea what to say, and he throws up his hands and says, "We cut off her hair." Then he has to be told by the interrogators that she was shot in the head.

That is such a classic sequence that I have seen dozens of times, in dozens of cases, where somebody has been made to think that it is in their best interest to do what these cops want, trying to give them the story they want, and just can't come up with it because they weren't there. It's so classic.

Q. I have worked with mentally challenged kids before around Brendan's age, and I can totally see when watching "Brendan's confession" on *Making a Murderer* how Brendan wanted to help those officers come to their conclusion. That's why he was throwing out those guesses. I have worked with those kids, and that's what they want. They want to be able to help.

A. Yes, they want to please the authorities exactly. That's what I always say about this case. You don't have to be a lawyer to kind of get what's going on with Brendan. You need to be a parent, maybe a mom or dad or teacher or a neighbor or somebody who knows someone like Brendan.

After the series came out, I had the very good fortune of being able to travel around the globe to talk to people about *Making a Murderer* and wrongful convictions and Brendan's confession. Wherever I spoke literally across the globe, people would come up to me afterward and say, " I know someone like Brendan, I have a Brendan in my life, and my heart broke when I saw him doing that, just trying to please these older authority figures." You know it's Brendan himself who moves people.

Q. Why wouldn't the court have appointed someone to sit in on the interrogations with Brendan? To leave a sixteen-year-old who has challenges in an interrogation with trained detectives for hours on end. It doesn't seem fair. Why can't there be somebody else there who is on Brendan's side to try and help level things out there?

A. I think leveling it out is exactly the right phrase. It was obviously not a level playing field when you got any kid, let alone one with disabilities like Brendan. Here's the interesting thing and something not a lot of people know. Only about thirteen of fourteen states require police right now to try to contact a parent before questioning a child. So, in the vast majority of states, there is no requirement that a parent gets notified. That's something we're working on changing very much. I'm a mom. I've got two boys, and I would be horrified to find them being questioned, to be put into legal jeopardy without my knowledge. But that happens in a lot of these cases.

But you are also right that sometimes a parent's protection isn't enough. You know parents are susceptible to these types of interrogation tactics just like their kids are. The reform that we really push for at the center of wrongful convictions is to require a lawyer to be in the interrogation room for kids. Now, this was law in zero states before *Making a Murderer*. But after the world saw what happened to Brendan, I am pleased to say that two states so far, Illinois and California, have passed the first laws in the country requiring lawyers in the interrogation room for certain kids. Those are baby steps, but they are long overdue to protect all of our kids.

Q. You started doing a *Wrongful Conviction* podcast. Why was that?

A. It, again, had everything to do with *Making a Murderer* when those filmmakers showed up in Brendan's case and started filming him in court. He didn't solicit it. He didn't ask for it. And he had no idea who they were until they told us they wanted to make a series about it. When the series was released years and years later, we didn't expect it to light the world on fire the way that it did. Suddenly, after working on Brendan's case for nine years, the world was saying his name. The world had that same transformative moment that I had when I was a law student. Right there, watching the same videos and saying this is not right, and what can I do to help and to make sure that this doesn't happen again?

I saw how this Netflix series had transformed the way that so many people thought about the criminal justice system and the way that it interacts with people who are maybe not rich or powerful or well connected. I thought to myself that if Brendan's story can energize people this much for a change, I've got a lot more stories like that. Stories that are just as engrossing, just as fascinating, just as disturbing, and just as motivating. To get people organized and people calling for action, calling for change, and getting people aware of some of what their rights are.

That's what led Steve Drizin and me to create our podcast, *Wrongful Convictions and False Confessions*. We've worked on so many of these false confession cases that have videos from inside the interrogation room that is just like Brendan's, sometimes even worse. So, we use that real interrogation video to tell twelve stories of false confessions. Of people who were manipulated into falsely confessing in the interrogation room, who was convicted on the basis of those confessions and sometimes, over the course of years, even decades, have fought and fought for the truth until they were finally exonerated?

Q. What are the criteria that you use in order to decide which cases will be used in the podcast, or have you investigated them?

A. If I could just step back and answer as a lawyer, at our Center of Wrongful Convictions, we get about three thousand five hundred letters every year. They are from all around the country, and they all say that they are wrongfully convicted. And they say that they are innocent and ask us to look into their cases. But there are only five of us at the center, so we can take very few cases. We are a pro bono organization, and we don't charge anyone whom we represent. Steve and I have never charged Brendan or his family a nickel for the work we have done on his behalf. We're proud of it, frankly.

So, we are very careful to pick cases not only where we believe in someone's innocence but where we think we can really help and where there's something we can actually do to make a difference. You wouldn't believe the cases that come across our doorstep. It's not a case of just sort of magically me being able to discern somebody is innocent when other people haven't been able to.

We have cases come to us where people confessed during interrogation. People who have confessed to rape and murder. Then the DNA from the rape victim's body was tested before trial, and it excluded them definitively, and they were convicted anyway on the basis of their confession. That's usually a pretty good sign that that case is worth looking into.

We had a case like that a few years ago, the Dixmoor Five. It was a case of five teenagers who were interrogated about the rape and murder of their fourteen-year-old classmate. They were all interrogated, and three of them ended up confessing and implicating the whole group, and they all go down for this crime. But before any of this went to trial, the DNA from this rape victim was tested. And it was not any of the five teenagers. But, they still go down based on the confessions and spend close to twenty years in prison before a couple of other Innocent organizations around the country, and we decided to take their cases.

At that point, we took the DNA sample from the victim and ran it through the National DNA database, which didn't exist twenty years ago. And we got an exact match to a single adult male, a repeat sex offender, who lived a couple of blocks away from the victim. He had a history of raping and attacking other women, including this fourteen-year-old girl. It's signs and signals like that when the case just doesn't make sense. Especially when the scientific evidence doesn't make sense, that is what makes you at least take a second look at a case.

The Dixmoor 5 were five African-American teenage boys, Robert Taylor, Jonathan Barr, James Harden, Robert Lee Veal, and Shainne Sharp, who was convicted in 1991 of raping and murdering fourteen-year-old Cateresa Matthews. Three of the accused boys gave confessions to detectives, which led to all five of them being convicted of the crime. After their trials, the boys each claimed that they were hit and beaten during their interviews with police, but no appeals were heard, and they remained in prison.

In 2011, DNA recovered from the murder scene was tested, and all five of the convicted boys didn't match. Instead, a previously convicted sex offender, Willie Randolph, did match. After this, the five men filed suit alleging that police had kept that DNA evidence from their lawyers, and their convictions were vacated on November 3, 2011.

It took another five years before Randolph was charged with the rape and murder of Cateresa Matthews. In 2014, the wrongly convicted men received forty million dollars in a settlement with Illinois.

Q. Does the podcast *Junk Science* interfere in trials and even sometimes get a suspect convicted? And if so, how hard is the recovery from such a conviction?

A. It's really interesting when you get into the criminal justice system and start reading about cases, trial transcripts, and police reports. The real sort of nuts and bolts of how our system works. There are so many things that we think are true about forensic science and, frankly, the functioning of the criminal justice system. So many things that we all think are true that it turns out to be sort of based on myths or old information. Outdated information.

A great example is we all believe that no one would falsely confess. But now we are learning this happens way more often than we think. Junk science is another really good example. Josh Dubin has a series of shows, also on the *Wrongful Conviction* podcast, which is about junk science. He brings on experts who deconstruct a lot of the scientific evidence that is used all the time in jury trials. Things like blood spatter evidence or gunshot residue evidence. The kind of stuff we are hearing about on CSI. But it turns out there are more and more reasons to question the accuracy of a lot of this kind of evidence.

Josh Dubin is a famed defense attorney and ambassador to the Innocence Project, which produces and hosts the *Wrongful Conviction: Junk Science True Crime Podcast.*

The Innocence Project

Wrongful Conviction: False Confessions Podcast

Wrongful Conviction: Junk Science Podcast

Listen to the full interview with Laura Nirider on my website:

https://www.alanrwarren.com/
hom-podcast-episodes/
episode/7493052c/laura-
nirider-wrongful-convictions

Part Four

THEN THERE'S THIS?

As with any true crime murder case, there have to be rumors that abound. Anytime you investigate this type of case, you have to interview as many people as possible, not only the detectives, doctors, or any professionals involved but family, friends, and coworkers of both the victim and suspects. The more people you talk to will give you a more comprehensive big-picture view of the setting and scene of the crime before, during, and after. This approach is an integral part of the investigation and helps to decide what is possible and what could happen, and what is not.

It's pretty amazing what kinds of stories you might hear. And even though some of the stories seem really bizarre, you have to take them seriously enough to do a follow-up or some research on the possibilities.

Another perspective I can give you about this that might help you to understand what I'm saying would be to picture yourself at the center of a murder investigation. Whether you make yourself the victim of the murder or the suspect doesn't matter, the choice is yours. Once you've decided who you are in the crime and what the crime was, it's time to do our investigation. So, step out of yourself for a minute and put yourself as an investigator – a person nobody in your life knows. This part is vital to this experiment, and you'll see why shortly.

At the beginning of your investigation, you need to find out who the victim was, what kind of work they did, and who their family and friends were. Once you get that basic information, it's time to find and interview everyone connected to the victim. So, put yourself as the victim. Imagine our investigator approaching everybody connected to you – your spouse, children, family, friends, people you worked with, and more. Can you imagine what each of those who know you would say about you? This is where it all begins—

the rumors and reasons that somebody murdered you.

These stories take up a detective's precious time during an investigation while trying to find the real culprit. Remember that each tip has to be investigated. But there's also a different kind of rumor or story that might not be so personal to the victim or the suspect. For some reason, these have become the focal point of the news over the last ten years and to the heights of networks actually running miniseries covering the rumor or conspiracy.

Chapter 9
Interview with John A. Cameron

During the Winter of 2015, even though the new crime docuseries *Making a Murderer* was all the rage among the true crime community, I still had a crime show to make, and not every episode could be on the Steven Avery case. A serial killer case that had been making a few waves was that of Edward Wayne Edwards. I had never heard of him, so the new book written by John A. Cameron had the perfect title, *It's Me, Edward Wayne Edwards: the Serial Killer you Never Heard Of.*

This case was especially interesting to me because the killer Edwards had once been on the television game show, *To Tell the Truth*, which was then, and still is, one of my favorite game shows ever. Not only was Edwards convicted of killing five people, but he remains the suspect in up to a dozen more murders. So, I thought this would be a great case to cover on the show. Unbeknownst to me, it was about to become much more of a case and more popular than I had expected, not because of the killings we knew about by Edwards, but the killing we didn't know.

Edwards' murder case was examined in Cameron's book, which was released in the Winter of 2015, the same as *Making a Murderer*. Cameron retired from the Great Falls Montana Police Department in 2005, where he worked as a sergeant of detectives who worked the cold cases of the state. Cameron had successfully worked with the FBI task force to help capture the child cannibal killer Nathan Bar-Jonah.

After leaving the police department, Cameron went to work for the corrections division in Montana. While working at the Deer Lodge Prison in 2010, he met Edward Wayne Edwards, who had been imprisoned there after he was convicted of being a serial killer. During this time, Cameron got to know Edwards and learned much more about what caused him to commit such awful crimes.

It was this information that led to Cameron completing the book and having it published. I should make you aware that Cameron would add new sections to the book over the years and rerelease it again. Each section would usually be dedicated to another killer that had made the news and been arrested, but Cameron would explain to the readers that the real killer was Edwards.

I interviewed Cameron three or four times from 2015 until 2019, usually coinciding with the latest released edition of his book on Edwards.

By now, you are probably wondering why this chapter on Cameron and his work on Edwards is in a book covering the *Making a Murderer* docuseries on Netflix and the Steven

Avery and Brendan Dassey murder cases. It's included because, in the second interview that I had with Cameron in early 2016, he claimed that, in fact, Steven Avery or Brendan Dassey had nothing to do with Teresa Halbach's murder. The real murderer was Edward Wayne Edwards, and he could prove it.

Edwards was not the only person ever accused or rumored to have been the real killer of Teresa Halbach. But it was undoubtedly the most prominent one. This claim would lead to a new edition of Cameron's book and several news programs. It eventually even led Cameron to get his own cable television series covering the Avery murder trial and all of the murder cases he was saying Edwards did.

According to Cameron, Edwards liked to set people up for murder. He would observe his victim and watch them for a while to get to know their habits in daily life. Once he was ready, he would move in and kill his victim and make sure that somebody else was made to look like the killer. He even went as far as to go to their trial to watch the innocent person get imprisoned for his crime.

Cameron also believed that he saw Edwards in the courtroom during Steven Avery's trial while watching one of the episodes of *Making a Murder*. His appearance at the trial is what started Cameron to link Edwards to the Avery case.

The following is a compilation of the three interviews with questions relating to the Teresa Halbach murder case. Again, like the other interviews used in this series of books, they are all available in their entirety on our website.

Q. I think we should start with Edward Wayne Edwards and who he was, and what he has done in the past so that we can later understand his connection to the Halbach murder case.

A. In 2010, I was working in Deer Lodge Prison in Montana as a Parole Board Analyst, and I was a retired police detective for twenty-five years prior to that. In 2010, a serial killer named Edward Wayne Edwards got caught in Wisconsin for the first time for murder, and he was seventy-six years old. He was married, had five children, and had eleven grandchildren.

While I was working in Deer Lodge Prison, I was notified that Mr. Edwards had been in Great Falls, Montana, in 1956, and that's where I live, in Great Falls, and that's where I had been a police officer. I had a cold case of a couple who were parked in a "lover's lane" in 1956. They had been kidnapped and then executed. It remained unsolved forever until Edwards was caught in Wisconsin in 2010, where he had confessed to killing a couple on a lover's lane there in a similar fashion. So, that began my investigation of Edward Wayne Edwards in June 2010.

Q. How did Edwards finally get caught?

A. Well, what happened was Edwards, at the age of seventy-six, finally gets identified as being a serial killer when his daughter turned him in after she was watching a cold case. She remembered that when she was very young, her father had taken her to the scene of a double murder. It turns out that scene of a double murder was a Wisconsin double murder that he actually confessed to in 2010.

So now, at the age of seventy-six, he's identified as a serial killer, and they put out a memo to all agencies, especially to agencies that were connected to a book the man wrote. Edward Edwards wrote a book when he was thirty-nine years old. It was an autobiography of his life, and he claimed that he was a reformed criminal and now was a happily married family man.

But what it turned out to be was that he was a big con artist, and he used his wife, his family, and his children as alibis as he traveled the country, killing for his entire life. He was married three times. So, when I was able to put him in Great Falls in 1956 at the time of our double murder, I just decided that I was going to write him a letter and ask him if he would confess to that murder so that we could at least tell the relatives that he was in prison and that he was actually going to be executed.

That ended up becoming a six-year-long investigation now on a serial killer that started killing at twelve years old in 1945 and never stopped until 2009. His entire M.O. was to set other people up, and he did it in practically every part of the country and every decade since 1945.

Q. Who was his first killing when he was twelve?

A. His first killing was on June 5, 1945, in Chicago. He broke into a woman's house, who was about thirty years old, beat her to death in bed, drowned her in the tub, put tape on her body, and also wrote on the walls, "Please stop me. I can't control myself. I'm going to kill more." Prior to this, he had been in a Catholic orphanage where he had been abused and had just escaped from it.

It was like he was killing his mother in the first few killings, over and over again. His mother had been shot in front of him when he was very young. After he was abused, he just took this to the "dark side" at age twelve.

Q. What kind of book did he write?

A. What he claimed his book was, was his metamorphosis from being a really bad apple to being a family man, and it was published in 1972 at the age of thirty-nine. But, what the book ended up being was a puzzle of murder. Inside the book, he had put an entire chapter of Great Falls, Montana, my hometown, where he killed a couple. He actually detailed the killing of the couple in parables throughout the story, and that ended up being true for the whole book.

He traveled the country after he wrote this

book and killed everywhere that he spoke about being in this book and set people up. The book was one big murder game thrown in the face of society as a taunt to show how smart he was. The reason he titled it *Metamorphosis of a Criminal* is all that it really meant was the metamorphosis of a serial killer. He metamorphosized into the best killer ever; that was his goal. Edwards's goal was to have the highest kill count of any serial killer and be the evilest serial killer there ever was.

Q. You say he liked to set others up for his killings. So, was he proud when he was able to kill someone, then set up someone else for the crime, and then watch them get convicted? Did that make him happy?

A. That's entirely what the whole book was about too. He called it a "crime of recognition." When I first got involved in this investigation, Mr. Edwards told me he was into crimes of recognition, and he had mentioned in his book that he was into them. I never understood what he meant by that, but because what everybody thought was, if you're into crimes of recognition and you're a killer, then why don't you stand up and admit everything that you did? Especially when he finally got caught in 2010?

But that's really not what he meant by "crimes of recognition." What he loved to do was kill somebody, set somebody else up, and then watch. Every day he could sit at the coffee table with his wife and his kids around and read a story about one of his murders that somebody else was going down for it.

He was able to set somebody up in 1946, and that meant that he (the wrongful man convicted) spent his entire life in prison until 2012 when he died an innocent man in prison set up by Ed Edwards. So, by age thirteen, he was so good at setting people up that that became his addiction for the rest of his life.

He just loved to sit back and attend the funerals of the victim and appear in documentaries about the murder. He was always standing in front of everybody under an assumed identity and just gloating at what he created.

Q. How did that work with him always having a family and wife? Were they not aware of his life of killing, or was he not living with them?

A. When I first started this investigation, I was working on the 1956 murder in Great Falls. Then, he was married to a woman named Jeanette, who was eighteen years old and from Idaho Falls. He actually kidnapped her in 1955 and took her all over the country while he killed them, portraying himself as a doctor of psychiatry, a police officer, and a preacher with a wife who was pregnant.

She dared never to cross him. I interviewed her in 2011, and for the last sixty years, she never told anyone what happened during the eight months of travel she did with him in 1955 and 1956 for fear that he would kill her. He ended up spending his entire life taunting her with letters and threats that if she ever told anybody, he'd kill her son. They had a son that was conceived in Great Falls. I got to interview that son, who is fifty-nine now. All he knew about his father was what his mother had told him, that he was a serial killer and a horrible man, and she never wanted him to know anything about him.

Q. How did Edwards find his wives?

A. His M.O. was to kidnap a girl, forcing her to basically travel the country with him and be under his control, impregnate her and kill the entire time portraying himself as a happily married man. That ended up proving true when he married again in 1968. He was married to his wife for the last forty-four years and had five children and eleven grandchildren. They basically traveled the country, and he would kill in adjoining states as he moved them around in campgrounds.

Q. Did Edwards have a particular type of person that he wanted to kill? A certain age, hair color, or look that he went for?

A. He was a ritual killer, and he created ritual murders. What I mean by that is all of the murders tie together in some element. Whether he's killed one, three, or six at a time, and he has done that, he stages his murders as rituals usually based around Satanism or Catholicism. His victims are of all ages, all types, and all colors. He shoots them, stabs them, burns them, strangles them, and has cannibalized them.

He wasn't like most serial killers with sexual

addiction. His addiction was to kill. And to kill in a manner that would set someone else up and create a crime of recognition that would get into history and would be talked about forever.

What's the profile of a serial killer like Edward Edwards? The FBI didn't have one. Nobody actually realized the man really existed. He taunted us his whole life with different identities, and his M.O. was just to kill and set people up.

Q. What did you mean when you said earlier that Edwards taunted everyone with the murders?

A. Edwards was a letter writer his whole life. What he would do was kill, then he would send letters to the police or the victim's family or the editors of newspapers. And the letter he sent would have stories and true information about the murders, and it would be kind of a taunt to authorities by saying the real killer is the guy writing the letters. It's me.

Q. What happened to Edwards?

A. He died on April 7, 2011, in an Ohio jail. He had been captured in Wisconsin in 2009 for a double murder. He pled guilty to it and then realized that he couldn't get his death penalty, and that's what he always wanted if he was caught. He wanted to be executed.

So, he called the Ohio press in 2010 and confessed to another "lovers lane murder" in Ohio, hoping to get the death penalty. Then he found out that he couldn't get the death penalty for the one he confessed to because the Supreme Court had put it on hold that year. So then, he was forced to confess to one more murder. A murder of a twenty-five-year-old man in Ohio, whom he had befriended, adopted, changed his name and insured him for $250,000. He then kidnapped him, beheaded him, held his body for six months, and then planted his body around Christmas time in a cemetery to collect the $250,000. He didn't get caught in that murder for thirteen years and collected the $250,000 in 1997. It's with that money he traveled the country, killed people, and set people up until 2009.

Q. You were just in Wisconsin, and you have gotten involved with the Steven Avery murder case of Teresa Halbach recently. How did you get drawn into this case, and why?

A. Yeah, I have never even heard of Steve Avery until about three weeks ago. I published my book actually two years ago tomorrow. Since the publication of my book, I've been really busy investigating other murders that Edwards had done all over the country and setting people up. And working with people in prison to try and get them out.

Recently somebody contacted me and said you need to see the Steve Avery documentary by Netflix called *Making a Murderer*. So, I turned it on somewhere around Christmas Eve, and by the fourth episode, I couldn't believe what I was watching. That documentary basically showed what Ed Edwards was capable of doing behind the scenes when he set people up on all of the setups and how officials acted, and it just created hatred among everybody.

Most people are just starting to hear about the Steven Avery case. He was set up for murder on Halloween 2005 after he had spent eighteen years in prison for an assault that he didn't do. So, just prior to Edwards setting up Steven Avery, Avery was all over the press, and they were making laws in his name in Wisconsin. He was famous because he had spent eighteen years in prison, and he was innocent.

They were making a law in his name, and Edwards decided to steal his recognition and set him up for murder. It was only because of Steven Avery's name and that Avery is part of the Zodiac case. Steven Avery owned Avery Salvage and lived on Avery Road, and was the longest-serving convicted man in the public in 2003, 04 and 05. That's when Edwards decided to target him and to set not only him but set the police up.

Q. Now, you claim that Edwards is seen in the documentary series. Whereabouts is that?

A. Well, whether or not that's Ed Edwards in the documentary, there's an episode six in the Netflix *Making a Murderer*, and at twelve minutes and thirty-three seconds into the video, there is a shot of a man in a blue sweater standing by the door behind the prosecutor, and it lasts about five seconds. That is the first shot that caught my attention. That possibly could be Ed Edwards. Edwards loved to kill somebody, set someone up, and then attend the trial or attend the funeral, especially if there were cameras. If he could get himself photographed without anybody knowing the real killer was there, he would do it.

So, in the *Making a Murderer* shot in episode six, it's just a very strange shot, and it fits every aspect of Ed Edwards. I went out to Manitowoc last week and visited with the Avery family and tried to visit with the Manitowoc County Sheriff's office and have been trying to identify that man in the video to see if anybody knew him that attended the trial, and I haven't been able to find anybody yet.

Q. What kind of reaction did you get when you were there? Like by the Sheriff's Office or law enforcement?

A. Well, that was interesting. I thought for sure if I tried to call for a week straight after I watched the documentary and realized that Ed Edwards was the culprit. I called and left messages, but nobody would return my call. So, I really just popped in my car and drove fourteen hundred miles to Wisconsin and showed up at the Manitowoc Country Sheriff's office last Tuesday and tried to speak to somebody. They wouldn't accept my book, they wouldn't accept my information, and they didn't want to hear it. That's how it went.

That's how this has always gone regarding Ed Edwards because Ed Edwards was an informant his whole life. He knew police officers everywhere. He was friends with police officers everywhere, and once he got identified in 2010 as a serial killer, there were police officers everywhere that recognized him and went, "Ah geez, it's him." That's who he was, he was that man who knew them all. But they didn't know that he was a serial killer.

Q. How did the Avery family react to you and your theories?

A. I pulled into the salvage yard, and I spoke with Doloris (Steven's mother), Allan (Steven's father), Charles (Steven's older brother), Earl (Steven's youngest brother), and Brenda. I stopped inside the salvage in the office there. You know, the prosecutor in *Making a Murderer* kept saying, "How could somebody get Steven Avery's DNA and then plant it?" That salvage yard office had more DNA of the Averys in it. It would be easy to get anybody's DNA of the Avery family. You know it's a salvage yard. You cut your fingers daily. Your hands are completely dirty. You've got rags lying around that your bloody hands are on. That's how Edwards got the DNA of Steve Avery. It was as simple as grooming his way into the salvage yard. At the time, he was seventy-three years old. He was almost the same age as Steven Avery's parents, and he would have been harmless. They wouldn't have even known what he was up to. Just to get a little bit of blood and sweat. DNA is as simple as a t-shirt of Steve Avery's that he wore. The prosecutors made it sound like it was impossible to do.

Q. Do you have the scenario worked out of how he committed the murder of Teresa Halbach?

A. Yes. Steven Avery was released on September 11, 2003, and that was a very important time because just shortly after Steven Avery was released from prison after serving eighteen years, the police arrested two innocent men for one of Edwards' Halloween murders in 2001 in Columbia, Missouri. On Halloween 2001, Edwards killed an editor of a major newspaper in a parking lot. Then two years later, two innocent men, Ryan Ferguson and Charles Erickson, went down for the murder. Charles Erickson confessed just like Brendan Dassey did, and it was a false confession.

But all of this occurred just after Steve Avery was released from prison. Then, another Halloween murder of Ed Edwards ended up in a wrongful conviction, and that was the 1975 murder of Martha Moxley. In 2003, right around the time when Steven Avery was released, Michael Skakel lost all of his appeals. He was arrested and spent his life in prison for that murder. He's since been released for that murder. Ryan Ferguson has been released.

Both of these Halloween murders were committed by Ed Edwards. As soon as Steve Avery was released and all of these Halloween murders were in the press is when he decided to target Steve Avery for setup. So, it was as simple as grooming his way into the life of Steve Avery. Then finding a woman who would be coming to that salvage yard on a regular basis that he could kill and then set Steve up for it. That woman happened to be Teresa Halbach, who would go there on a regular basis and photograph for *Autotrader Magazine*.

So, she became the victim. She was the right

age, twenty-five, and she was attending a parish in St. Johns, Wisconsin, so everything matched with the Catholicism that Edwards liked to target to kill. Then killing her on Halloween night. She was not burned in that fire pit. Ed Edwards had blown bodies apart and burned bodies to bits his entire life and always had a preplanned disposal site. They would plant the body at a later date to whomever they wanted to lead it to.

Q. What was the significance of the date, Halloween, on which he murdered?

A. The significance of his occult thinking is Halloween is the dark side. And the day that follows Halloween in Catholicism is All Saints Day. The day that follows All Saints Day is All Souls Day. Those were the three days that Teresa Halbach went missing and was reported missing on All Souls Day, and that's just tying it to his Satanic cult nature. He's killing on the dark side on Halloween, which goes into the light side on All Saints Day. That's the only reason that he killed on those days. It was all ritual. He also killed on Christmas, Easter, the fourth of July, Memorial Day, Columbus Day,

Palm Sunday, and Good Friday. It was always tied into a date that would create more recognition. If you have a murder on Christmas, it's going to get more press than if it happened on June second.

Q. So, can you describe how Edwards got a hold of Halbach and killed her, then burnt her and placed her ashes in Avery's fire pit without anybody seeing him?

A. First of all, the murder had to happen on Halloween. So, that marine van that Teresa was going to photograph, somehow Edwards got wind that she was going to be there on that day. Or he implied it into somebody's mind that that would be a good day to have her come out and take the pictures. Somehow, she was designed to go there that day and designed to be seen by Steve Avery last because that's the only way it would work. If Steve Avery was the last person that she was seen alive, then he becomes a suspect.

So, it was simple as he knew she was going there to photograph at two-thirty, and that was the time that she showed up. That area is so rural. I just drove there. It's at least a quarter mile from the main highway into the salvage yard. Then the salvage yard itself is forty-four acres. So, it's a massive area and very rural.

All Edwards would have had to do was be on the side of the road, just down the road off the entrance to the salvage yard. That's an old man needing help, that's it. What the ruse was, we'll never know. But it's just as simple as an old man flagging you down that needs help.

Teresa was shot in the left temple, and she was also shot in the back of the head. So, she was the driver, and that's exactly how he would have done it. Walk up to the driver's window with a twenty-two, then pop one in the head, and a twenty-two does not go through for the most part. It goes into the brain and zips around, and kills you instantly. Push her in and drive away.

She wasn't reported missing for three days, so he had three days with that vehicle and her, and nobody even knew she was gone. On the fourth day, the Avery family went to their cabin. They left town and went to the cabin. The only one there was Earl, and that's the day that he planted the car, the bones in the fire pit, the bones in the barrel, and the cell phone in the barrel. Everything he planted there, Edwards had done exactly like that in 1955 before he went to Great Falls and killed there. He had committed a murder exactly like Teresa Halbach in California in 1955.

It was that simple. He knew Steve Avery would be having a big bonfire because it was Halloween night. It's just what they did – sit around and drink beer and have a bonfire. That body was blown to bits by a bomb, and Edwards detailed how he makes his bombs. Basically, he takes a body. He goes into the forest with the body, where he finds a log on the ground. That's a dense log. Digs a hole under the log and fills it with gravel. Fills it with ammonia nitrate. Puts the body on top between the log and the hole and sets it off. It blows the body to bits. That's what he did to a body in 1960 in Portland, Oregon. Then he just collected the remains and threw them in the fire pit.

Q. Edwards must have had access to Avery's trailer in order to get Avery's rifle, which he had hanging over his bed on the wall, as the prosecutors claim that Halbach was shot in the head with Avery's rifle.

A. That whole gun issue was kind of interesting because they didn't find the slug until March of 2006. Right there tells you what happened there. Did he shoot her with Steve Avery's gun? Because the slug would have been inside Teresa Halbach—her head—and Edwards would have collected it. Edwards was a civil patrol expert, and he groomed his way into searches for his own victims. In the case of Teresa Halbach on the day of the fifth, the people that searched for Teresa Halbach's car and walked directly to it were part of a volunteer search group at St. Johns Church. Over one hundred people. And that's what Edwards would have groomed his way into. He steered them to go right to the car as they went to go search. The lady who found the car said that God led her to the car, and she had attended the church just before finding it. I am sure that God did lead her to the car, but it wasn't God. It was Ed Edwards.

Q. The police didn't want to take your book, hear any of your evidence, or even talk with you either, did they?

A. Yes. Well, it's a shame that the police don't want to hear it now because, in a way, Ed

Edwards actually gives them kind of a break. They come across as really bad in that documentary, and they did some things that are horrible. The confession of Brendan Dassey is horrible and should have never been taken. It was clear that it was forced, and it wasn't proper.

But the planting of the keys in the house, later on, the blood in the car, and the DNA on the hood latch were all done by a serial killer that was designing it to make the cops look like they were doing it. The cops were all over the press before the murder. They were all being deposed because some of them were lying, and some of them were doing things that weren't very good.

They were about to pay out $36 million to Steven Avery, so part of the plan wasn't just to set Steven Avery up but to set the cops up too. That's what he did in all of his cases. It was about making the cops look like fools.

Q. How did the Avery family respond to your theory on the killing of Teresa Halbach and your suspect Edward Wayne Edwards?

A. Yes, they did. It was a great talk, and then the next day, they had a call from Kathleen Zellner, the famous attorney out of Chicago, whose now going to represent Steve Avery. Kathleen Zellner is in my book on page 392 because she represented Ryan Ferguson. So, it was really good to see her hop in on the case. I think she will run with it and get him out.

In September 2013, author and journalist Brian D'Ambrosio released a book called *Free Ryan Ferguson: 101 reasons Why Ryan Ferguson Should Be Released*, which was published by Jabberwocky Press. After its update in 2017, we interviewed D'Ambrosio on the show. During our talk, he never once mentioned having found any connections or having any suspicions of Ed Edwards ever having been involved in the crime or the wrongful conviction trial. Instead, he blamed the police and even the judge for his incarceration for coaching a witness to identify Ferguson at trial.

Q. Do you really believe that? Avery is really up against the wall this time.

A. Yeah, they all are. The thing about Steve Avery is he is just one of over a dozen men sitting in prison right now on Ed Edwards' murders that are in the exact same position. But they're not getting all the recognition that Steve Avery is right now.

Things that we know!

What were we actually able to find out about Edward Wayne Edwards? And what could we actually confirm about what he did as far as murders during his lifetime?

Edwards was born in Akron, Ohio, in 1933, where he grew up in an orphanage that he would later claim was physically and emotionally abusive. He joined the U.S. Marines as an escape from the orphanage but went AWOL almost immediately and ended up being dishonorably discharged. From there, he traveled around the country working odd jobs and ended up in jail for minor offenses such as robbing a gas station or corner store. In 1960, Edwards was named the prime suspect in a gas station robbery, arson, and murder. In 1961, he ended up on the FBI's "Most Wanted" list.

In 1972, Edwards wrote and published his book *The Metamorphosis of a Criminal: The True Life Story of Ed Edwards*. In October of that same year, he appeared on the popular evening television game show, *To Tell the Truth*, where he claimed to have never committed the murder that he was charged with back in 1961.

At the time of Edwards' death on April 7, 2011, at the age of seventy-seven, he had been convicted of five murders and suspected of fifteen others. He was arrested in 2009 for multiple murders while living in Louisville, Kentucky, and by 2010, he pleaded guilty to four murders.

The first couple he murdered was 21-year-old Billy Lavaco and his 18-year-old girlfriend Judith Straub, both living in Ohio. Straub's car was found parked at the Silver Creek Metro Park on August 7, 1977, with her shoes and purse left in the backseat. The next day police started a search at the park, eventually finding the couple dead. Both had been shot at point-blank range with a 20-gauge shotgun.

The second couple he murdered was 19-year-old Tim Hack and 19-year-old Kelly Drew, both from Jefferson, Wisconsin, which became known as the sweetheart murders. The couple was murdered in an area known as a place for couples to go to be romantic. Both were stabbed and strangled.

Edwards' daughter, April Balascio, believed her father was involved, and she went to the police. When questioned, he denied involvement. And with no evidence, they let him go. The case went cold. But in 2010, police had the DNA results from the crime proving Edwards' connection to the murder. Balascio would be the center of an A&E documentary in January 2018 called *People Magazine Investigates: My Father, the Serial Killer*. In this film, she claims that her father committed the sweetheart murders. She said he was very dark and that he made them watch several videos about the Zodiac Killer, who she also believed her father was.

This documentary would later lead to a six-part A&E series, but this time John Cameron was at the center of the theories. In the series, Cameron took Edwards' daughter's theory of her father being the Zodiac Killer and ran with it. Not only did Cameron believe that Edwards was Zodiac, but he also added more murder cases, such as the Black Dahlia, Jon Benet Ramsey, Martha Moxley, Laci Peterson, and several more famous murders. It even went as far as Cameron telling me in one of our interviews that he thought Edwards also murdered Marilyn Sheppard in 1954 to frame her husband, Dr. Sam Sheppard. The murder of Dr. Sam Sheppard's wife had national media attention and led to several movies and television series about the case.

It should be mentioned that we covered both the Sam Sheppard and Martha Moxley murder cases on our show. We had Sheppard's attorney, F. Lee Bailey, on the show for the Sam Sheppard case. For the Moxley case, we had Michael Skakel's cousin, lawyer, and author of the book, *Framed,* Robert F. Kennedy Jr. Both interviews are also available to listen to at Robert Kennedy Jr. - Framed - House of Mystery Radio on NBC | Acast & F Lee Bailey - OJ Simpson Trial Lawyer - House of Mystery Radio on NBC | Acast Neither Kennedy nor Bailey had any belief in Edwards having been involved in either murder.

One year later, in 2011, Edwards also confessed to the murder of his twenty-five-year-old foster son, Dannie Boy Edwards, to collect an insurance policy of $250,000. Edwards traveled to his son's house in Burton, Ohio, where he shot him in the face twice and buried him in a shallow grave. Edwards was sentenced to the death penalty for this murder.

John Cameron has created a website where he outlines the details of Edwards' life, and the people Cameron believes were killed by Edwards. His claims do not have any direct evidence linking Edwards to most of the murders; however, you can find them here at 1933-1949 - Cold Case Cameron.

Only one other set of murders was linked to Ed Edwards from someone other than John Cameron—the Beverly Allan and Larry Peyton murders in Portland, Oregon, in 1960. According to author Phil Stanford in his book *The Peyton-Allan Files*, he believed that Edwards might have committed the murders and possibly set up two others to take the fall. Both were initially convicted but later released even though law enforcement strongly believed they were guilty.

Also, it was later confirmed that it was not Ed Edwards in the courtroom who was caught on film during the *Making a Murderer* series on Netflix. Steven Avery's latest lawyer Katherine Zellner responded to Cameron's claims about Edwards being Halbach's murderer to *Rolling Stone* magazine, saying, "I have had nightmares that make more sense. Edwards would not have had the opportunity to kill Teresa Halbach. She would not have pulled over for him. He did not have her schedule that day to know where she would be at a particular time. Edwards also did not have access to or familiarity with the Avery Salvage Yard in order to plant the evidence." Zellner also mentioned that he was seventy-two years old at the time of Halbach's murder and would have been too old and frail at the time to have committed the murder.

Listen to the full interview with John Cameron on my website:

https://www.alanrwarren.com/
hom-podcast-episodes/
episode/922aba7f/john-a-
cameron-ed-edwards-set-up-
steven-avery

Part Five

INTERROGATION OF BRENDAN DASSEY

Chapter 10
The Interrogations of Brendan Dassey

Throughout all of the interviews covering this case, and with the general public via the internet and media, the arguments around this case always came down to the Brendan Dassey interrogation. On March 1, 2006, police detectives brought sixteen-year-old Dassey into the Two Rivers Police Detachment to be questioned about the murder of Teresa Halbach. This interview was videoed by the police, which was a common thing for them to do – not only for murder interviews but even less severe cases like petty theft or writing bad checks. I'm sure police had no idea then that this video would be watched by over 500,000 people on the internet years later. Or that it would be the basis for

Netflix's *Making a Murderer* series for the defense of Dassey. Or that it would create an absolute hell storm for all law enforcement who were involved.

The prosecution's Ken Kratz claimed that about thirty minutes of this video had been removed and not shown on either the Netflix series or *YouTube*. Kratz contended that those 30 minutes were so crucial that if those 500,000 people who watched the edited version saw the original uncut version, they would change their minds entirely and support him and the conviction of both Dassey and Avery.

If you remember, in my interview with Kratz, he claimed that at the time of the interrogation of Dassey, he was being questioned only as a witness and not a defendant. He claimed that initially, the police had no idea or even thought that Dassey was involved in Halbach's murder. Rather, they felt that he might have seen something over that Halloween evening when she disappeared from Avery's property. Kratz claims that if you watch the beginning of the interview of March 1, 2006, you'll see that the officers were trying to find out what, if anything, Dassey saw that night while he was visiting Avery for the bonfire.

It wasn't until Dassey admitted involvement in the murder that the detectives began to look at him as a possible suspect. They then decided to change the tactic of their questioning to what is known as the "Reid Method." This method is widespread within the United States, and everyone learned what the process entailed after this case became popular. There would be some adverse reactions to the Reid Method, but it wasn't significant to the outcome.

Kratz contends that Dassey gave out information and the detective's methods changed during the thirty minutes that were cut from the interrogation video. He also believes that the Netflix series filmmakers deliberately manipulated their viewers into believing that both Avery and Dassey were innocent.

Was I, like all of the other viewers of this interrogation video, tricked into believing false information? The answer to that question was the first thing I wanted to find out.

During our interview with Kratz, he also claimed that he had the uncut part of the video interrogation of Dassey and had it posted on his *YouTube* page. I went to look, but it wasn't there. So, the search began. On the internet, there are hundreds of posted Dassey interrogation videos from March 1, 2006, but none of them had that missing 30 minutes Kratz mentioned. The next best thing for me was to get the interrogation manuscript stamped and filed by the court and read that over to see what exactly had happened in that missing time.

Reading the March 1, 2006 transcript, I noticed a strange thing. After Detective Wiegert read Dassey his Miranda rights, he started with this line of questioning:

WIEGERT: Um, I just, one question I had for you real quick, Brendan is, um, those jeans that Tom had talked to you about the other night with the bleach stains on 'em, do you still have those?

BRENDAN: Yeah.

WIEGERT: Where are those?

BRENDAN: They're at my house.

WIEGERT: Do you know where in your house they would be?

BRENDAN: Yeah.

WIEGERT: Where would they be?

BRENDAN: They're by the kitchen table.

WIEGERT: By the kitchen table, like laying on the floor or on an I looked at 'em and then put 'em on a chair.

It wasn't that I thought the question was necessarily bad. When the detective said, "Those jeans that Tom (the other detective in the interrogation room) had talked to you about the other night," I wondered, had they interviewed Dassey before this? If so, when and what happened during those interviews? Did the detectives interview Dassey for being a witness to the murder during those as well?

I soon found out that, indeed, those same two detectives interviewed Dassey not once but twice before this March 1st videoed interview. Time to get those transcripts now as well.

On February 27, 2006, the detectives went to his high school in the late morning and interviewed him for a couple of hours in one of the school's board rooms. And then, after contacting his mother, they took him down to the

Two Rivers detachment and interviewed him again.

I needed to start at the beginning. I needed to see the first time the detectives began to question Dassey to see how things progressed and to see if they treated him as a witness for both the first two interviews and the much-famed third interview on March 1st.

In all, there were four interviews of Brendan Dassey by Detective Mark Wiegert and Special Agent Tom Fassbender. The first two interviews were both done on February 27th. The first one started at about 10:30 a.m. at Brendan's high school and finished by about 2 p.m. The second interview picked up later that day, about 3:30 p.m., at the police detachment with Dassey's mother, but she never sat in on the discussion. The third interview, and the one that was videoed, happened on March 1, 2006. It was again at the sheriff's office. There were two more interviews with Dassey: one on May 12, 2006, with Detective O'Kelly, and the fifth interview the day after, on May 13, 2006, with both of the original detectives, Fassbender and Wiegert.

The following is what I picked out as essential points of view and hopefully answers what my guests had told me during their interviews with me. Transcripts of the first three interrogations of Brendan Dassey are on my website so that you can read them over in their entirety. Here are the links:

1. Interview #1 (at High School, Feb. 27, 2006)
2. Interview #2 (at Police Station, Feb. 27, 2006)
3. Interview #3 (at Police Station, March 1s, 2006)

Interview #1

Reading through interview number one with Dassey, held at his high school on February 27th, and the second interview later that day in the police station, it's obvious by the questioning that detectives suspected him of being part of the murder, or at least helping Avery conceal it. This belief is probably why in the third famous interview on March 1st, detectives started with the question about Dassey's bleach-stained jeans.

The interview transcript makes Kratz's claim about the third interview less genuine. The prosecution's claims about their method of interrogating Dassey in the first two interviews and at the start of the third interview, which was filmed on March 1st, as him to be only a witness is invalid. They had long decided before the March 1st interview that Dassey was involved in the murder of Teresa Halbach. Below I list some of the highlights which I think prove this.

From Page 441:

FASSBENDER: "No. Brendan, we know that, that Halloween and stuff you were with him and, and helped him tend to a fire and stuff like that behind the garage and stuff and, anything that you saw that night that's been bothering ya? And if you built the fire, and we believe that's, that's where Teresa was cooked. And if you were out there by the fire and stuff, and by your own words you went and got that, that seat out of a, the vehicle seat remember that one, brought it over and someone put it on the fire, did you put that seat on the fire or him?"

BRENDAN: "We both did."

FASSBENDER: "What did you both grab it and put it, put in the fire? What did you see in the fire?"

BRENDAN: "Some branches.........a cabinet, and some tires."

FASSBENDER: "Did you see any body parts?"

First, I found it strange that Fassbender said, "That's where Teresa was cooked." But the excerpt above and below reveal that right from the start of interrogation number one on February 27th, Dassey was at least considered a witness to the clean-up of the Halbach murder.

From Page 442:

FASSBENDER: "...They're talking about trying to link Brendan Dassey with this event. They're not saying that Brendan did it. They're saying that Brendan had something to do with it or the cover-up of it, which would mean Brendan Dassey could potentially be facing charges for that. And Mark & I are both going well ah he's a kid, he had nothing to do with this, and whether Steve got him out there to help build a fire and he inadvertently saw some things, that's what it would be; it wouldn't be that Brendan act-actually helped him dispose of this body. And I'm looking at you, Brendan, and I know you saw something, and that's what killing you more than anything else, knowing that Steven did this, it hurts. Whether it was an accident that Steven did it by, however it happened, he's, he's gotta deal with that. Truthfully, I don't believe Steven intended to kill her. I don't know how it happened. Only Steven knows how it happened, and potentially you. Do you know how it happened? What did you see in that fire?"

BRENDAN: "............some black...............some garbage bag on there."

FASSBENDER: "Uhm, and what was in the garbage bag?"

BRENDAN: *no answer.*

FASSBENDER: " ....garbage bag, and they were plastic? Plastic melts pretty quickly, right?"

BRENDAN: "Well, I would burn garbage."

FASSBENDER: "Where did you get those bags from?"

BRENDAN: "………..from his garage … he was saving it for a bonfire"

FASSBENDER: "mm huh."

BRENDAN: "Cuz we invited some friends over, but they canceled."

Eventually, the seasoned detectives got Dassey to say that he saw clothing on the fire and even some blood on them. He would also admit to Avery getting the clothing they burned from his garage. Then Dassey claimed the most damaging thing he saw was a toe and something that looked like a forehead of a human with a little bit of flesh on it.

From Page 456:

WIEGERT: "Now I've been told that you and STEVE talked about the body in there. OK, that's what I was told, and I believe that. You guys did talk about it, didn't ya?"

BRENDAN: "Yeah."

WIEGERT: "What did he tell you?"

BRENDAN: "That I shouldn't say…"

WIEGERT: "OK. So you tell me how that conversation went. What did you say to him?"

BRENDAN: "I said, why did you do it because…………and he's like……………and told me not to say nothing."

WIEGERT: "Did you know who it was?"

FASSBENDER: "Did he say who it was?"

From Page 458:

FASSBENDER: "Let's back up to when you go out there, did he tell you about Teresa right away, or did you actually see the body before he told you?"

BRENDAN: "I seen the body."

FASSBENDER: "And he knew you saw it. Did you say something to him then, or did he say something to you?"

BRENDAN: ."…..is what he said………"

WIEGERT: "And he also said what?"

BRENDAN: "He got angry and stuff"

WIEGERT: "And what else did he say?"

FASSBENDER: "Did he say how it happened, it's important.

FASSBENDER: "I can't believe that he wouldn't have told you how it happened and how did he kill her….."

BRENDAN: *no answer.*

WIEGERT: "How do you know that?"

BRENDAN: "Because....................."

WIEGERT: "I also-heard that he told you how he did it, that's that's true isn't it?"

BRENDAN: "Yeah"

WIEGERT: "Tell me what he told you."

BRENDAN: ".......car... the... jeep..."

WIEGERT: "What did he tell you he did in the jeep?"

BRENDAN: *no answer.*

WIEGERT: "Where's the knife that he used to stab her?"

BRENDAN: "In the truck, under the seat."

From Pages 464 & 465

WIEGERT: "I have to ask you another difficult question. It's very important that you to be honest with me. OK? Did you have anything to do with the death of Teresa Halbach?"

BRENDAN: "No."

WIEGERT: "Tell me who did."

BRENDAN: "Steve."

WIEGERT: "And Steven did it by how again, tell me that again."

BRENDAN: "That he stabbed her."

FASSBENDER: "OK. Had he told you that? Yes or no?"

BRENDAN: "Yes"

FASSBENDER: "Did he say he had had a gun with a .... at all?"

WIEGERT: "Did you ask him about a gun? And he told you that he did this in her truck?"

BRENDAN: "Yeah."

WIEGERT: "And he tied her up first?"

BRENDAN: "Yes."

WIEGERT: "And then he stabbed her inside the truck."

BRENDAN: "Yeah"

This interview finished at 2:15 p.m., and they let Brendan return to his Science class. They phoned his mother, Barbara, at her job and told her to come to the school. Once she arrived, they explained to her what Brendan had told them and said that after he finished his class, they were taking him to the sheriff's office to do some more questioning and would like her to be there.

After Brendan finished his class, he returned to the board room where the detectives were waiting. They had him write a statement of what he had told them earlier that day. You will also read in the full transcript online that they had to help him a lot, not just with spelling but with remembering what he had told them. The detectives then took him and his mother to the police station. They again read him his rights and asked his mother to sit in on the interview, but she refused.

It looked as though the second interview was to try and get even more information about what happened at the Avery residence on the night of October 31, 2006. Just with the few excerpts included above, they had reason to believe that Dassey knew about Avery killing Halbach. And that he even knew that she had been burned that night on the bonfire at Avery's place. But was Dassey involved in the murder?

This train of thought would be the natural direction for the detectives to look. In the second interview, there was only detective Wiegert asking Dassey questions. Throughout almost two hours, Wiegert focused on what Brendan saw in the fire and how Avery killed Teresa. He just tried to have Dassey elaborate in more detail but wasn't very successful.

Like in the first interview, the detectives had to suggest much for Brendan to say. This fact could indicate a few things: Dassey didn't remember what detectives were trying to get him to talk about, or he was very introverted and had no social skills, or he felt so pressured by the detectives to try and make up something so that he could finish and go home, that when one of the detectives gave a suggestion when they asked him a question, he responded by using that suggestion as a crutch to answer the question.

The Missing Part of the Third Interview on March 1, 2006

In the third interview with Dassey, the questioning method started just as the previous interviews went. Kratz claims this interview style is that of a witness. But from the excerpts included above from the first two interviews, I'm afraid I have to disagree. I believe that they were, in fact, using the Reid technique and interviewing him as, at the very least, an accomplice to the murder and disposal of Halbach's body.

One thing I can agree with Kratz was the sudden additional information about the rape and murder of Halbach by Dassey, which at the very least, confirmed to detectives that he was involved in both. I have placed the critical points of the interview where Dassey admitted to what they both did to Teresa and how they did it. During this crucial part of the interview, neither of the detectives gave Dassey leading information and therefore looks valid. Therefore, the only reasonable challenge to Dassey's interview would be his mental capabilities and not having a lawyer or parent with him at the time.

From Page 550:

WIEGERT: "Now, let's be honest. What did he tell you? What did he show you?"

FASSBENDER: "What did you see, and what did he tell you?"

BRENDAN: "He showed me the knife and the rope."

WIEGERT: "Where was she? Come on we know this already. Be honest."

BRENDAN: "In the back of the jeep."

WIEGERT: "She was in the back of the jeep?" (Brendan nods "yes") "Was she alive or dead at that time?"

BRENDAN: "Dead"

FASSBENDER: "Are you sure?" (Brendan nods "yes") "OK. What did you see in the back? Now, this is hard, but what did you see in the back of the jeep?"

BRENDAN: "That she was laying there with like a small blanket over her."

FASSBENDER: "Do you remember where her head was?"

BRENDAN: (shakes head "no") "Not really."

FASSBENDER: "Did she have clothes on?"

BRENDAN: "Yeah." (nods "yes")

FASSBENDER: "She was clothed."

BRENDAN: (nods "yes") "Yeah."

WIEGERT: "Was she tied up already? Or did you help him do that?" (Brendan shakes his head "no")

BRENDAN: "She was tied up already."

FASSBENDER: "Where? Tell me how she was tied up."

BRENDAN: "Like the rope was right here around her body."

From Page 565:

BRENDAN: "I knocked on the door, and he answered it."

WIEGERT: "Yeah, and then what?"

BRENDAN: "I gave it to him, and then I left."

WIEGERT: "Come on now. You just heard screaming over there."

FASSBENDER: "You're making this hard on us and yourself."

WIEGERT: "Be honest. You went inside, didn't you?" (Brendan nods "yes")

From Page 566:

FASSBENDER: "Yeah."

WIEGERT: "You went in the trailer?"

BRENDAN: "mm huh." (nods "yes")

FASSBENDER: "You're noddin'."

WIEGERT: "OK. Did he invite you in?"

BRENDAN: "Yeah."

WIEGERT: "OK, and where was she?"

BRENDAN: "In his room."

WIEGERT: "OK, did you go back there and look?"

BRENDAN: "No." (shakes head "no")

WIEGERT: "Brendan, be honest."

BRENDAN: "I didn't."

WIEGERT: "How do you know she was in his room?"

BRENDAN: "The door was open."

WIEGERT: "Could you see her?"

BRENDAN: (nods "yes") "Yeah."

WIEGERT: "Was she alive?"

BRENDAN: "Well, she was handcuffed to a thing."

WIEGERT: "She was handcuffed to what?"

BRENDAN: "The bed."

WIEGERT: "Was she naked?" (Brendan nods "yes") "Was she alive?"

From Page 567:

BRENDAN: "Yeah."

WIEGERT: "How do you know?"

BRENDAN: "Cuz she was moving around."

WIEGERT: "Was she making any noise?"

FASSBENDER: "It's aright bud."

BRENDAN: "Yeah."

FASSBENDER: "What was she sayin'?"

BRENDAN: "Screaming for help."

WIEGERT: "What was handcuffed? Her hands or her legs or both?"

BRENDAN: "Both."

WIEGERT: "And what were they handcuffed to?"

BRENDAN: "Like the hand, like there are round poles on each side."

WIEGERT: "OK."

FASSBENDER: "Of his bed?" (Brendan nods "yes") "And you, your, you're getting there, OK. Let's back up again, and did you go get the mail?"

BRENDAN: "Yeah."

FASSBENDER: "When you went to get the mail with your bike, did you hear somethin' at that time, or did it happen when you came back with the mail?"

FASSBENDER: "You can do it. Just tell us the truth."

BRENDAN: "When I came back."

From Page 570:

WIEGERT: "It's OK. Tell us what happened. What did he say to you?"

BRENDAN: "That he never got some of that stuff, so he wanted to get some."

FASSBENDER: "Never got what?"

BRENDAN: "A girl."

WIEGERT: "OK."

FASSBENDER: "What'd you say just a second ago, though?"

WIEGERT: "Repeat what you said."

BRENDAN: "That he wanted to get some."

FASSBENDER: "Some what?"

Brendan: "Pussy."

WIEGERT: "That's what he said to you?" (Brendan nods "yes") "OK."

FASSBENDER: "Now I can start believing you, OK?" (Brendan
    nods "yes")

From Page 575:

FASSBENDER: "And you had intercourse with her?" (Brendan nods "yes")

WIEGERT: "What does intercourse mean to you?"

BRENDAN: "That you stuck it in her."

WIEGERT: "Stuck what in her? It's OK."

BRENDAN: "My penis."

WIEGERT: "Where did you stick it?"

BRENDAN: "In her vagina."

WIEGERT: "OK." (pause). "How many times did you do that? How long did it take?"

BRENDAN: "Five minutes."

WIEGERT: "OK. What did you do after that?"

BRENDAN: "Put my clothes back on."

WIEGERT: "OK. Where is Steve at this time?"

BRENDAN: "Standing by the door."

WIEGERT: "What does Steve do then?"

BRENDAN: "Told me I did a good job."

From Page 576:

FASSBENDER: "There was nothin' covering her mouth?" (Brendan shakes his head "no") "Did she ask you not to do this to her?"

BRENDAN: "Yeah."

FASSBENDER: "Tell me what she said."

BRENDAN: "She told me not to do it so and told me not to do the right thing."

FASSBENDER: "Which was what?"

BRENDAN: "Not, not to do it and tell Steven to knock it off."

FASSBENDER: "Did she ask you to do anything else for her?"

BRENDAN: "To uncuff her."

FASSBENDER: "Go ahead. Anything else?" (Brendan shakes his head "no") (pause) "Were these things she was saying to you while you were doing this act?"

BRENDAN: "Yeah"

FASSBENDER: "Was she kinda sayin' it softly or loud enough or what?"

BRENDAN: "Well, she was cryin' an."

FASSBENDER: "OK."

WIEGERT: "After you're done, and you put your clothes on, what happens next?"

From Page 580:

FASSBENDER: "What does he tell you he's going to do at, this time, you're goin' back to the bedroom?"

BRENDAN: "That he was gonna tie her up, stab her and then choke, like, choke her and that."

FASSBENDER: "He told you this?"

BRENDAN: "Yeah."

FASSBENDER: "And you went with him."

BRENDAN: (nods "yes")

FASSBENDER: "He went into the bedroom, what does he do? Again the video, you see it, I know you see it, what does he do?"

BRENDAN: "That he gr, he grabs the rope that was on the side of the bed, tied her up, stabbed her like this and jumped on her, and started choking her."

FASSBENDER: "Is she fighting at this time?"

BRENDAN: "She's trying ta move away."

FASSBENDER: "Is she saying anything?"

BRENDAN: "Screaming."

WIEGERT: "You helped to tie her up, though, didn't you? (pause) Brendan, cuz he couldn't tie her up alone, there's no way. Did you help him tie her up?"

BRENDAN: "Yeah."

WIEGERT: "OK. Tell me what you did."

From Page 586:

WIEGERT: "What did he make you do, Brendan? It's OK, what did he make you do?"

BRENDAN: "Cut her."

WIEGERT: "Cut her where?"

BRENDAN: "On her throat."

WIEGERT: "Cut her throat? When did that happen?"

BRENDAN: "Before he picked her off the bed?"

WIEGERT: "So she was alive yet, right?" (Brendan nods "yes")

WIEGERT: "So she's alive, and you cut her throat?"

BRENDAN: "mm huh."

WIEGERT: "Was that before or after Steve stabbed her?"

BRENDAN: "After."

WIEGERT: "It was after Steve stabbed her?"

BRENDAN: (nods "yes") "mm-huh."

WIEGERT: "Was she a-how do you know she was alive?" (pause) "Tell me. When you cut her throat, how do you know she was alive?"

BRENDAN: "She was breathing a little bit."

Dassey's Rights in the Interrogation Room

We heard Laura Nirider address this in her interview with us. Not only was she concerned that the discussions took place without anybody in the room to help Dassey out, but many of the interviews also contained suggestions or fed information to Dassey. Can a detective conduct the same kind of interview technique with an adult? Well, it seems that they can.

It is almost always legal for law enforcement to lie to suspects during interrogations. Police can also make false claims and even tell the suspect that they have witnesses that saw them commit the crime or that they have their DNA or fingerprints at the crime scene. They can even claim that the suspect's friends had confessed to being part of the crime and said they were all in on it together, including the suspect.

According to Nirider, these are the powerful psychological tools linked to some of the false confession cases she has covered in her time with the Innocence Project. The numbers are surprisingly high, as Nirider claims that of the 268 cases involving children who were wrongfully convicted where their cases got overturned, 34 percent of them confessed to these practices during their interrogation. But it's a long road to travel to try and have a case overturned for a false confession. In America, detectives are allowed to use these practices on anybody interrogating, including children.

The other legal question Nirider raised during our interview was that Dassey had no legal counsel or parent in the room. Again, this is another one of those cases where the only rights allowed to minors are the same rights allowed to adults: Miranda rights. The interrogation is legal as long as police read the minor's Miranda rights and ensure that the minor understands those rights. Usually, the issue regarding children and interrogations is that once they've been read the Miranda, the little ones think that they are under arrest and believe they have to answer any questions. They don't. It's within their legal right to say nothing and ask for a lawyer. Would a minor know enough about their rights and be confident enough to do this?

The question for the Dassey case is, "Did Brendan have the intelligence to understand his rights?" This question has been another big battle fought online over this case. In August 2016, an appeals court ruled that Dassey's confession had been coerced, involuntary, and unconstitutional and ordered that Dassey be released from prison. After that, the Wisconsin Justice Department filed an appeal to that ruling, and Dassey's release was blocked until a decision was made.

In June 2017, the Seventh Circuit had a three-judge panel that upheld the original decision that overturned Dassey's conviction. Still, the Wisconsin Justice department again appealed and asked the Seventh Circuit panel to hear the appeals case. After the entire board listened to the case in December of that same year, they decided to uphold Dassey's conviction. Nirider took this case to the Supreme Court, but they refused to hear the case. Dassey will remain in prison, with his first eligible parole date in 2048.

References

1. https://www.nickiswift.com/480978/the-truth-about-steven-averys-ex-wife/
2. https://archive.jsonline.com/news/crime/judge-in-avery-case-closes-evidence-hearing-b99643078z1-363822531.html/
3. https://graziadaily.co.uk/life/tv-and-film/teresa-halbach-real-victim-making-murderer/
4. https://archive.jsonline.com/news/crime/judge-in-avery-case-closes-evidence-hearing-b99643078z1-363822531.html/
5. https://archive.jsonline.com/news/crime/avery013007-b99643075z1-363822431.html/
6. https://archive.jsonline.com/news/crime/evidence-allowed-in-avery-trial-b99643071z1-363822271.html/
7. https://archive.jsonline.com/news/crime/judge-to-allow-blood-comparison-b99643067z1-363822121.html/
8. https://archive.jsonline.com/news/crime/sheriffs-agencys-role-muddies-avery-case-b99643065z1-363822061.html/

9. https://archive.jsonline.com/news/crime/steven-avery-trial-begins-da-says-blood-bone-link-avery-to-killing-b99643042z1-363821141.html/

10. https://archive.jsonline.com/news/crime/nephew-implicates-avery-b99643036z1-363820531.html/

11. https://www.thefamouspeople.com/profiles/brendan-dassey-43093.php

12. https://en.wikipedia.org/wiki/Making_a_Murderer#Private_investigators

13. http://coldcasecameron.com/killers-timeline/1933-1949/

14. https://madison.com/edward-wayne-edwards-a-timeline-of-his-life/article_1604863a-741b-11df-ae59-001cc4c03286.html

15. https://www.pajiba.com/tv_reviews/did-ed-edwards-frame-steven-avery-for-the-murder-of-teresa-halbach-.php

16. https://www.rollingstone.com/culture/culture-features/inside-one-mans-serial-killer-unification-theory-630621/

17. D'Ambrosio, Brian: *Free Ryan Ferguson: 101 Reasons Why Ryan Should Be Released* ASIN: B00F35AA2K, Jabberwocky Press; 1st edition, September 9, 2013

18. Kennedy, Robert F.: *Framed: Why Michael Skakel Spent Over a Decade in Prison for a Murder He Didn't*

Commit ASIN: B01EEQ9B4G, Skyhorse
Publishing, July 12, 2016

19. https://madison.com/wsj/news/local/
crime_and_courts/article_48ae9dfa-6245-11e0-
9e72-001cc4c03286.html

20. https://abcnews.go.com/TheLaw/Diabetes/
elderly-con-man-admits-murdering/story?id=
10877100

21. Cameron, John A.: *IT'S ME: Edward Wayne Edwards,
the Serial Killer You Never Heard Of* (First ed.). Santa
Rosa, California: Golden Door Press. pp. 76–79.
ISBN 9781885793058, 2014

22. https://www.wave3.com/story/10829261/
louisville-man-arrested-in-wisconsin-cold-case-
double-murder/

23. https://www.cleveland19.com/story/12633629/
convicted-killer-pleads-guilty-to-slaying-a-norton-
couple-in-1977/

24. https://www.cleveland.com/metro/2010/06/
convicted_murderer_edward_edwa.html

25. http://www.dailyunion.com/news/
article_c5a783f2-f943-11e7-9f3a-
bb88a0f9ade9.html

26. https://www.cleveland.com/metro/2011/04/
convicted_serial_killer_edward.html

27. http://www.dailyunion.com/news/
    article_69bd0238-0a56-11e7-a499-
    4bf127661e89.html

28. https://pamplinmedia.com/pt/9-news/38808-
    after-50-years-murders-still-a-mystery

29. https://www.youtube.com/watch?v=
    PoU9MvdqVfo

30. https://www.cbsnews.com/chicago/news/
    dixmoor-5-sue-over-wrongful-rape-murder-
    convictions/

31. https://www.chicagotribune.com/news/ct-xpm-
    2011-11-03-chi-prosecutors-vacate-convictions-in-
    91-rape-slaying-of-dixmoor-girl-20111103-
    story.html

32. https://www.chicagotribune.com/news/breaking/
    ct-dixmoor-five-arrest-met-20160831-story.html

33. https://web.archive.org/web/20111113075330/
    http://www.innocenceproject.org/Content/
    Background_on_Dixmoor_and_Engle
    wood_cases.php

34. https://www.chicagotribune.com/news/breaking/
    chi-isp-agrees-to-pay-40m-to-five-wrongly-
    convicted-of-dixmoor-rape-murder-20140624-
    story.html?track=rss

About the Author

Alan R. Warren has written several bestselling True Crime books and has been one of the hosts and producers of the popular NBC news talk radio show the *House of Mystery,* which reviews True Crime, History, Science, Religion, Paranormal mysteries that we live with every day.  From a darker, comedic, and logical perspective, he has interviewed guests such as Robert Kennedy Jr., F. Lee Bailey, Aphrodite Jones, Marcia Clark, Nancy Grace, Dan Abrams, and Jesse Ventura. The show is based in Seattle on KKNW 1150 AM and syndicated on the NBC network throughout the United States, including on KCAA 106.5 FM Los Angeles/Riverside/Palm

Springs, as well in Utah, New Mexico, and Arizona.

Read more about Alan on his website:
alanrwarren.com

Also in the VOICES OF CRIME series

The *House of Mystery Radioshow* has been on the air for ten years, broadcasting in over a dozen cities in the U.S. It started as a way to interview guests knowledgeable in many of the world's mysteries involving crime, science, religion, history, paranormal, conspiracies, etc.

The *Voices of True Crime* series is a curated collection of interviews about true crime from the show. Each volume focuses on an actual criminal case, or several, providing the background and reproducing the main points discussed in the interviews. Like the *House of Mystery Radio Show Interviews* series, this book does not attempt to solve the case but only reviews it. There will be no committed answer at the end of the book. I aim to concisely review the extraordinary things learned during the show's interviews. These interviews are an excellent reference for researchers and a good overview for people who don't know the topic well. Similar to the other interview books I've published, only the highlights of each interview will be included. All these interviews and more are available to listen to on my website: www.alanrwarren.com/hom-podcast-episodes.

VOLUME 1: THE O.J. SIMPSON MURDER CASE

Volume 1 covers the O.J. Simpson murder case. Over the last century, there have been plenty of trials called "The Trial of the Century," but of all mentioned, the O.J. Simpson case rose well above the rest. The fact that the accused murderer was a high-profile athlete and celebrity was almost enough to reach that status, but then the brutality of the murders made the world stagger. Throw in the fact that modern technology allowed every aspect of the case to be televised worldwide, including the infamous slow-speed chase and his sensational trial, and it's no wonder this case achieved that title.

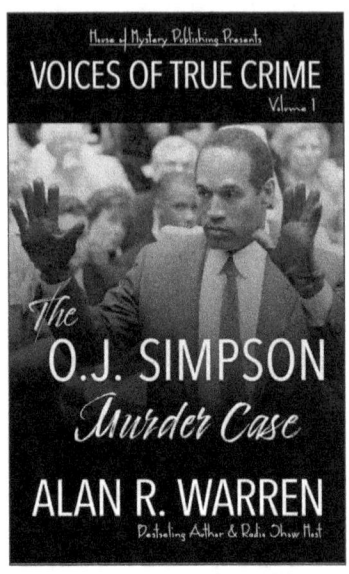

House of Mystery interviewed several key players involved in this case: Marcia Clark, the lead prosecutor in the trial; F. Lee Bailey, one of Simpson's "Dream Team" of lawyers; Kim Goldman, sister of victim Ron Goldman; Norman Pardo, Simpson's manager for 15 years who whole-heartedly believes a serial killer murdered Nicole and Ron; and Andy Caldwell, the detective who questioned and arrested Simpson for the robbery in Vegas. Online links to the actual interviews are included.

Also in the HOUSE OF MYSTERY INTERVIEWS series

The *House of Mystery Radio Show* has been on the air for ten years, broadcasting in over a dozen cities in the U.S. It started as a way to interview guests knowledgeable in many of the world's mysteries involving crime, science, religion, history, paranormal, conspiracies, etc. The *House of Mystery Interview Series* is a curated collection of interviews from the show. Each volume focuses on one of the mysteries, providing the background and reproducing the main points discussed in the interviews. There will be no committed answer at the end, as the Interviews series does not attempt to solve the case. Instead, it provides the most compelling aspects of each theory held by different experts. This series is an excellent reference for researchers and a good overview for those unfamiliar with the case. Online links to the actual interviews are included.

VOLUME 1: JACK THE RIPPER: THE INTERVIEWS

Volume 1 of the Interview Series, "Jack the Ripper," covers the ultimate "who-done-it" mystery of 1888 London. Scotland Yard's "Whitechapel Murder File," in which Jack the Ripper had a starring role, went cold before it could be solved. One hundred thirty-two years later, and the fascination with this cold case mystery continues. Ripperologists passionately debate suspects, opinions, research methods, and theories. Even which murder victims to include in the case is widely debated. Astonishingly, work continues, and today Ripperologists still find new clues that bring us closer to solving the mystery.

The mix of credible and diverse thinkers interviewed includes world-renowned historian Neil Storey, the Godfather of Ripper Research, Paul Begg, Ripperologists: Paul Williams, Tom Wescott, Adam Wood, and Steve Blomer. Michael Hawley contributes his unprecedented scientific approach to the case. Suspect Ripperologists Jeff Mudgett, whose great-great-grandfather was serial killer H.H. Holmes, weighs in, as does Russell Edwards, who believes he solved the mystery through DNA.

~

VOLUME 2: JFK ASSASSINATION: THE INTERVIEWS

the HOUSE OF MYSTERY RADIOSHOW presents

ASSASSINATION
THE INTERVIEWS: VOLUME 2
ALAN R. WARREN
Foreword by VINCENT PALAMARA

Volume 2 of the Interview Series, "JFK Assassination," covers *the* unrivaled historical mystery of historical mysteries. The JFK assassination is the grandfather of all conspiracies in America and arguably where they all started. A highly popular President with movie star looks and charisma, effecting significant changes in society, was brutally cut down in his prime. The official story was that JFK was killed by a sole assassin, Lee Harvey Oswald. However, many conspiracy theorists believe in an assassination plot involving the FBI, CIA, U.S. military, VP LBJ, Cuba's Fidel Castro, Russia's KGB, the Mafia, or some combination of those entities.

The research and interviewing of the JFK assassination experts lasted for over six years. Arguments and counter-arguments from a diverse mix of bestselling authors make for some interesting discussions. And some of the authors interviewed are considered just as controversial as the mystery itself. Most authors focused on who they believe was responsible for the assassination. Others narrowed their focus on certain related aspects, such as the Zapruder film, Nix film, Garrison Tapes, etc. All information collected from each expert adds value to the overall mystery.

VOLUME 3: ZODIAC KILLER: THE INTERVIEWS

Volume 3 of the Interview Series, "Zodiac Killer," covers another serial killer who has stayed in the spotlight for years after their case has gone cold. It's been over 40 years now, and fascination with the Zodiac is still going strong. Experts passionately debate Zodiac suspects, Zodiac''s letters/ciphers, opinions, and theories. Even which murder victims to include in the case is widely debated.

The diverse mix of authors interviewed includes cryptologist and cipher expert David Oranchak, authors who propose their suspects are already convicted serial killers, authors who claim the Zodiac was their father, authors who offer new or already considered suspects, and an author who argues the Zodiac killer didn't exist at all and that Zodiac was a hoax.

VOLUME 4: MYSTERIOUS CELEBRITY DEATHS: THE INTERVIEWS

Volume 4 of the Interview Series, "Mysterious Celebrity Deaths," covers interviews relating to the mysterious deaths of the influential rock band Nirvana's frontman Kurt Cobain, the 1960s mega-icon Marilyn Monroe, T.V.'s *Hogan's Heroes* lead actor Bob Crane, the talented and multi-award-winning actress Natalie Wood, and the people's princess, Princess Diana.

VOLUME 5: CONSPIRACY THEORY CULTURE: THE INTERVIEWS

Volume 5 of the *House of Mystery Interviews Series* will focus on theories that go against the scientific facts that we have learned over many generations of the human race. There is something uniquely intriguing about a good conspiracy theory. They tell tales of heroes, villains, and alternative realities. Conspiracy theories represent secret knowledge: real or not, and there is something very pleasing about having supposed insider knowledge.

the HOUSE OF MYSTERY RADIOSHOW presents

CONSPIRACY THEORY CULTURE

THE INTERVIEWS: VOLUME 5

ALAN R. WARREN
Foreword by Dr. JOSEPH USCINSKI

Because of their entertainment value, you can find conspiracy theories everywhere. Implausibility doesn't make conspiracy theories less entertaining. What if the moon landing was faked? Who would have been involved? How could they have pulled it off, and why? What if the earth is encapsulated by a celestial lid? What if the infamous leader of the Third Reich escaped Germany? What if President Franklin Roosevelt had allowed the Pearl Harbor attacks to happen?

These are a few of the conspiracy theories discussed in

this volume. As with the others in this series, this book will cover the most popular conspiracies – the ones that have gained lots of ground in the media and on the internet. Some of them even have celebrity followers. During the interviews, guests were shown the utmost respect, as we tried to find out their reasoning for believing what they do and how they developed their beliefs.

VOLUME 6: PARANORMAL & THE OCCULT: THE INTERVIEWS

During the first ten years of the *House of Mystery Radioshow*, the paranormal field was very popular in society, including several television series covering ghost hunting, haunted houses, mediums communicating with the dead, witchcraft, and even Satanism. Spirituality was also discussed since religion is often given the power to either protect or attack one doing the investigation.

In Volume 6 of *The Interviews* series, the shows relating to the Paranormal will be covered in two parts. Part 1 will cover topics relating to Parapsychology, Mediums,

Psychics, and paranormal tools such as Ouija boards and haunted items. Part 2 will cover religion, the occult, and topics such as Near-Death Experiences, Lucid Dreaming, Psychokinesis, as well as paranormal tools such as Astrology, Numerology, and Tarot cards.

The interviews selected for this book were chosen for the guest's believability and knowledge in their area of expertise.

their beliefs.

VOLUME 7: D. B. COOPER: THE INTERVIEWS

This book reviews the D.B. Cooper case. It is divided into five parts. The first part gives the bare facts we know about the hijacking. The second part covers the primary suspects listed according to the FBI, media, or public opinion, supported by the show's best interviews with authors and researchers who covered these suspects. The third part covers the other major suspects popular among the public but not considered Cooper by the FBI or law enforcement authorities. The fourth part covers some of the major suspects who came forward to police and confessed to being D.B.

the HOUSE OF MYSTERY RADIOSHOW presents

D.B. COOPER

THE INTERVIEWS: VOLUME 7

ALAN R. WARREN

Cooper. The last part is dedicated to the wave of copycat hijackings that occurred after the Cooper case. And there were quite a few.

www.ingramcontent.com/pod-product-compliance
Lightning Source LLC
Chambersburg PA
CBHW070920120626
46546CB00001B/333